Tending To Your Inner Garden

Lorraine,

Sending you love

+ magic as you

enter the Inner Garden.

Blessings in abundance,

Catherine xxx

Tending To Your Inner Garden

A Woman's Journey
Towards Wholeness

CATHERINE MAGUIRE

McZine Publishing

First published in Great Britain 2012

Copyright © 2012 by Catherine Maguire
Cover Design © 2012 by Gill Bradley

McZine Publishing Limited
6 Lancaster Lodge
83/85 Lancaster Road
London W11 1QH
www.mczine.com

A CIP catalogue record for this book is
available from the British Library

ISBN: 978-0-9574198-0-3
eBOOK MOBI POCKET: 978-0-9574198-1-0
eBOOK EPUB: 978-0-9574198-2-7

10 9 8 7 6 5 4 3 2 1

All papers used by McZine Publishing are natural,
recyclable products made from wood grown in well-managed
forests. The manufacturing processes conform to the
environmental regulations of the country of origin.

Printed in Great Britain by
CPI Group (UK) Ltd., Croydon CR0 4YY

For Pele

Thank you from the bottom of my heart for welcoming me into your Garden.

Contents

I am the Light,
I am the keeper of the flame,
I am the holder of the Heart Song,
I am the bringer of the dawn.
I am You,
And you are Me,
We are One,
In Spirit.

Preface

If you feel that you exude the deliciousness of feminine radiance from every cell of your being then I'm afraid this is not the book for you. If however, you desire a deeper connection to the rich feminine wisdom and sensuality that is your birthright, please, keep reading.

Tending to your Inner Garden is a practical step by step guide for women that draws on the ancient wisdom of shamanism and tantra to reconnect you with your feminine sacredness; your Inner Garden. Ancient traditions were well aware that women are intricately connected to the natural cycles and rhythms of the earth. When our heart pulses to our internal earth rhythm we come home to our exquisite nature. As women we spend a lot of time and money searching for our womanhood outside of ourselves. No matter how hard we try, the clothes, the job, the children, the lover or the husband will not fulfil us. Or maybe they will, but what happens when they are gone? When we connect with our Inner Garden we begin a magical love affair. We first learn to love ourselves deeply and wholeheartedly as women. We then learn to bask in the essence of our radiance so that we can have a passionate love affair with life.

The first part of the book will take you to the compost heap where you can gently and lovingly mulch any limiting beliefs or experiences that you have regarding your womanhood. You will then be guided to sow new seeds, and reconnect to the potentiality of who you can become. The second part of the book guides you through the Ten Stepping Stones to Wholeness. A beautiful process that provides you with the tools you need to grow and blossom. Interwoven through the book you will also hear my own story. A story of how I went from television executive, to breakdown, to finding the essence of my being in a cupboard under the stairs!

We are on the cusp of a new paradigm. We are being asked to become the conscious creators of our destiny. When we embrace our womanhood the power struggle between us and our men folk ceases to exist. We can take a new place beside each other as complementary forces instead of opponents in a war of the sexes. It is now time to accept that we are the Wise Women. We are the gateway to the Heart. We can birth a new world if we are first willing to birth ourselves. I invite you to join me in this amazing adventure.

In Deep Love,

Catherine Maguire

Introduction

On my journey to inner peace, self love, wholeness, or whatever your word is for personal healing, I have read many books, attended many classes, starved, purged, detoxed, and even walked over hot coals. I have cried, laughed, talked, and danced thinking that this next thing would be 'the one'; the one magical healing modality that would transport me to transcendence. Many of the spiritual texts say that it's not the destination but the journey that's important. Being a stubborn bullish Taurean, that never sat very well with me. I lacked the patience for it and just wanted to be happy. I desperately grasped for every 'this will change your life' book and workshop, like a drowning woman gasping for one more breath in the hope that the pain and self loathing would cease, and be replaced by the tranquil calm and strength that I had sometimes glimpsed within myself, but more often had read or heard about.

The truth is, if all the 'I can fix you in 10 easy steps books' or three months in an ashram retreats worked, we would only have to read one book or attend one mind blowing, ego shattering course, and hey presto we are transformed. We would be luminous beings who float around the planet vibrating to the frequency of unconditional love, able to heal ourselves, the world, and our fellow man. Unfortunately this is not the case.

What I have found, and this is a pretty big statement for the aforementioned bullish Taurean, is that our spiritual journey is like a jigsaw. Everything we do, every course we take, every book we read, every person we meet and every tear we cry are all pieces of this worldly puzzle. For the chosen few, it's like a kindergarten puzzle, only ten pieces and easy to put together. For the rest of us however it's more like a 1500 piece puzzle and a lot of the pieces appear to look the same.

We spend what seems like lifetimes trying to finish the puzzle and see the final picture. We first have to wrestle with frustration, disappointment, doubt, anger and exhaustion until we finally surrender, walk away and come back to it another day, and maybe day after day until in time it gets done. And then comes that fateful day when the end is in sight and because the universe, I am convinced, is so ironically hilarious, you get to the end only to realise that you have lost a piece along the way.

I have in time learned however that this apparent cosmic joke is the essence of the spiritual journey. To create something new there has to be death and transcendence. The egg and sperm have to cease to be, to create the miracle that is a child. Flour and eggs have to cease to be so that a delicious cake can be made, and for us to be, to truly be, we have to put to rest the parts of ourselves that no longer serve the whole, the oneness. And so back to our jigsaw, that one missing piece represents the sacrificial offering, something that had to be relinquished on the journey to the whole. And so it is with life.

On this journey I have had to let go of many aspects of myself including fear, loneliness, self doubt, shame, addiction, desperation, my fierce independence and pride. But what I have gained is so much more than I can list with superfluous adjectives, and believe me, I love superfluous adjectives. Ultimately where it has taken me is to a love affair with myself. I have always been a giver; you got a problem, I will fix you. You need a shoulder to cry on, here's some Kleenex. The list goes on. Finally I had to admit that I could give to everyone but not to myself. Shifting from giving to receiving is one of the hardest lessons I have undertaken so far.

In the following pages it is my heartfelt desire to guide you on your path to remember. To remember who you are and who you have the potential to become. Through stories, personal accounts, simple exercises and guided teachings I hope to ignite a flame within you. It is a flame that you will need to tend, to add kindling and breath to. Ultimately, I hope to provide you with a rich organic compost into which you will want to sow the seeds of your becoming. You can then allow that divine potential that dwells within you to bloom and flourish into a glorious colourful fragrant palette. So if you're ready come with me and let us take that first barefoot step into the dewy morning and out into the garden.

Woman as Garden

I magine a world where we honoured each other; where we honoured our gifts, our beauty and our potential. Imagine a world where prosperity in all its forms reigned and where there was peace. Imagine a world so filled with colour and lushness that each moment you gazed out into the world it took your breath away with its beauty. This world does exist, but we have worn it down, beaten it up and left it discarded waiting for something new to come along to stimulate us, heal us and revive us.

Think of a beautiful garden in whatever form it takes for you. Think of the seeds and the bulbs that go down into the earth and after a period of rest emerge to share their colour, their beauty and their radiance with the world. They provide the nectar of life; nectar to bee, bee to honey, honey to human; bringing sweetness into every moment.

Think about yourself, are you a radiant flower? Are you bringing your sweetness, your nectar into the world? Or has your stem become rotted, your bulb and seed diseased? Is the contribution you make to the world toxic as opposed to joyous?

If you are reading this book there is a longing in you. A longing to feel whole; a longing to bring your honey, your fragrance to the world. The journey is two fold. In finding your inner palette, your radiant inner garden, you heal. And in healing yourself you also heal the world. If you are at peace with yourself, the world around you is at peace. If you embody beauty, you will radiate it within and help it to flourish. If you are joyous, you spread those seeds far off into the distance so that many people can benefit from your positive charge.

This is a book of becoming. We all started as that beautiful seed or bulb full of infinite potential. That potential is our birthright; Spirit in all its glory bestowed it to us in his/her loving generosity. For whatever reason, that potential has been diminished, and we are left barren and often alone.

The journey to your inner garden is a journey to

wholeness. It is a journey to re-sow those seeds of becoming in new fertile ground so that they may flourish and blossom. The journey to your inner garden is a reconnection to the Divine Feminine that lives within. This is no arbitrary journey. The world depends on it. For the planet to heal, we must heal, and time is running out.

I once heard a story told to me by one of my teachers. He said an old South American medicine woman told him that the reason the rain forests were being cut down was because they represented the Divine Feminine. The rain forests are lush and dark and rich and moist. The power of the feminine has often been feared. Her intuitiveness, her strength and her rage have been captured in legends since time began. Her gentleness, her softness and her passion have won the hearts of men throughout time. So why is she feared? Why is she destroyed and why do we not honour the Divine Feminine within ourselves?

The answer to this story is old and complex. There are many versions of this story and one of them goes like this.

Once upon a time, back when the world was young. Men and women lived in joyous, loving harmony with each other. The men hunted, searched for new lands, and fended off dangers that prevailed over their tribe. The women nurtured the young, tended to the crops and complimented the harsher energy of the men with their softness and gentleness. The days were spent hunting and gathering and at night they would sit around the fire, put the children to sleep and tell great stories; stories of the day, stories of the spirit of the land, and stories of what had occurred in dreamtime the night before. And so they shared and together they guided the path of their tribe.

One day, for reasons no one really understands the world turned, and things started to change. The men grew fearful of the women's intuition. The women started to resent the strength of the men. Instead of living in harmony the tribe divided, and now instead of us as one, it became us and them. In an effort to maintain their righteousness the men tried to assert their strength over the women. They tried to curtail their time together and their freedom.

The women in return started to belittle the men. Instead of sharing stories of the great adventures of their men folk, they talked about how inadequate they were as husbands and mates. Fear and resentment grew. Men feared the power and capabilities of the women. They were the healers and they knew how to use the medicine herbs. What if they used the herbs to harm or poison them? Men were the hunters, what if they hunted out the women folk and punished them by death? Fear and terror reigned. And so it continued for many eons. Although men and women came together they never really trusted each other, or gave themselves over completely to love.

And all this time mother earth she cried. She cried for her children. She cried for the suffering she saw in their lives. And eventually she started to cry for herself. For not only had her children turned on each other but now they turned on her too. They poisoned her, polluted her and no longer honoured her as the birth mother of them all. They say the pain was so great that over time her heart broke and in an effort to protect what little of her self was left, she slept. She slept the great sleep in the hope that one day her children would reunite and once again walk the path of love.

She slept for many years occasionally stirring from her sleep to observe her children only to quickly return to her slumber. She saw her children realise that it was time for change and embrace the concept of free love. But free love was no love. It was a time of exploration, of expansion and of relinquishing prevailing social mores, but still the games played out and the distance between man and woman remained.

She watched as women in an effort to be accepted became more like men. They wore shoulder pads and power suits but this did not heal the divide.

She watched as men made objects of their women, separating physical from spiritual form. Women were there to give pleasure, but they were not to have a soul.

She watched as women tried to energetically castrate their 'new men', only to realise that they didn't want men to be like women but needed men to be like men. But the damage was done. Men wandered lost, cast adrift in an ocean of dishonouring, paddling frantically for friendly shores.

After many battles and much loss, man and woman sat once again side by side at fire. They recounted tales of all that had happened to them since they had separated from each other and from sacred union with the Divine. They cried and laughed together wondering how they had gotten it so terribly wrong. We are different, we are unique but we are complimentary, they realised. One is nothing, without the other. We are the yin and the yang. Together we are whole.

As they joined once again in sacred loving union, mother earth, overcome by the love her children had found once again for each other, woke up. She wrapped her children in her loving arms, forgiving them as only a mother can for their indiscretion. Knowing in her wisdom that they would not be so quick to separate again, her children had at last come home.

The time has come for us to honour ourselves and each other as a species. The world and its evolution now depend on it. I cannot be a teacher to the men folk and initiate them in the ways of the sacred masculine, for that has not been my journey. I do not carry that wisdom. And it would be arrogant of me to think otherwise.

I can however ignite the flame of womanhood and help you to reconnect to the Divine Feminine that lives within. The Divine Feminine is your Inner Garden. She is rich and moist and wet. She is passionate and juicy and intuitive. She is nurturing and she is giving. She is all loving and she is Divine.

Many women have forgotten their Inner Garden. They are instead a barren wasteland waiting to be transformed. That time has come. In the following pages there are stories and exercises that will help you unleash your beauty and blossom, so that you can reveal your true self to the world. Every journey, it is said, begins with the first step. In taking this first step towards embracing your womanhood, you heal for all the women that have gone before and for the children that have yet to come. You will unleash your potential, and your creative genius. You will unleash your ability to manifest and make whole.

The quest for the Divine Feminine that lives within us, is a multi faceted and, in many cases, diverse course in self awareness which eventually brings us to the place of Wholeness that we started out looking for. At times the quest can seem overwhelming and contradictory. However, the learning is in the quest itself. There is no fail safe method which will connect you to that lusciousness that lives within. There are many paths on the way to your temple and there are many different resources that you can employ. What I am endeavouring to do in these pages is to provide you with tools which on their own while interesting and insightful have limited potential. But joined together they create a beautiful palette of colour which will both help you heal, and transform your world.

Mother Earth no longer sleeps. She calls to her daughters and asks of us to help. Help her reunite her children; help her to teach them to open their hearts to love, and walk the beauty way.

The stepping stones within this book are a pathway to your garden. They are whole and yet they are not complete. They are whole in the respect that they provide you with a healing map. They are not complete in the sense that you must add your own colour and vibrancy to them and embody them as your own. The beauty of us all is that we are individual and unique. Stop and ponder for a moment. If you were a garden, what kind of garden would you be? A herb garden, a Zen garden or a rose garden? There are as many gardens as there are people in the world. None of them are more or less beautiful that the others, all hold their own unique beauty. So as you work through these pages and start to clear away the debris, don't expect your garden to look like anyone else's. It cannot, for it is yours. Honour your garden, and in honouring your garden you can honour yourself. Then and only then can we stand shoulder to shoulder with all of creation, and honour each other from a place of pure and Divine unconditional love.

When Rot Sets In

Two of my close friends have recently had babies. And while they struggle with lack of sleep, sore nipples and the demands of their newborn, I look at their infants and all I can see is divine perfection. We all come into this world as perfect; we are a joyous bundle of divine potential entering into the adventure called life. We have not yet been tarnished by the brush of low self esteem, fear, inadequacy, self loathing, or abuse.

I'm sure that no parent holds their child in their arms and tells them, "I'm going to mess you up so bad that you are going to spend the best part of your adult years in therapy, just so you can remember how absolutely

14

wonderful you really were to begin with." And yet at some insidious point, the rot sets in. It might be a throwaway remark from a parent or teacher, it might be something we see or experience but over time our sense that we are indeed perfection slowly slips away to be replaced by a dank musky rot that plunges deep into the very soul of our being.

I do not think that I had an extraordinary childhood, I was the eldest of six, my mom was a housewife and my dad was a farmer. We didn't have lots of money and like many families hand me down clothes and tight budgets were a fact of life. My dad had an interesting relationship with money, it always burned a hole in his pocket, when he got paid we would live like lords for a couple of days, and then back to basics for the rest of the month. My mother has a much more sensible approach to money and I always felt that she resented the lack of freedom and financial independence that came with marrying my dad.

In theory I should have had an idyllic childhood. We lived beside the farm, our house looked out on the beach, we had lots of fields to play in, and we had plenty of company. Yet when I look at photos of myself as a child there always seems to be a sadness lurking in my eyes. I don't know if it is insecurity, loneliness or vulnerability, but as an adult I always want to wrap that little girl in my arms and tell her that everything will be okay.

I was always incredibly sensitive, never quite under-standing the torrent of emotions that ran through my little body. As a family we were never great for talking, and talking about emotions or feelings was a definite no go area. I was a champion of keeping things bottled up inside so I never got to really understand or express how I was feeling. Now I can identify some of those feelings as loneliness and the feeling of isolation, of not quite fitting in and of not quite feeling good enough.

When I was nine, while taking a ferry to France for a family camping holiday, myself, my sister and two of my brothers were sleeping in our cabin. My mother, dad and my younger sister, were asleep in a different room. I woke up to find a man whom I had never seen before standing over me with his hand between my legs. He hadn't noticed that I had woken up. Did I scream, did I shout out? No.

Instead, for reasons I will never quite understand, I lay there frozen for a while and then silently hatched a plan. I pretended to wake up, moving my body and yawning loudly. He got a fright I assume, and ran out of our cabin. For some reason I looked up to see my sister in her bunk looking down at me and she said, 'I guess he was checking to see if we were ok'. I never told her what happened. I never knew if she knew, but what I did do was take that event, file it in a folder called 'Bad Dreams', and banish to deepest recesses of my mind. Anytime the memory would try to surface I would dismiss it quickly as a bad dream before it would get a chance to reveal itself.

So you are probably wondering why I say that I do not believe my childhood was extraordinary. They say in Ireland one in four children have been molested or abused, and I do think what happened to me was mild compared to the suffering experienced by so many. I only tell you this to highlight the fact that all of us, for whatever reason, have a story; a story of our wounding; a story of what caused our pain; a story of the day when the rot set it.

However, what I do find really interesting is how we are shaped by our story, our wounding, and our rot. For some of us we don the mantle of the victim. "I can't be in a relationship because, of how my mother, my father or my family treated me." "You will just have to tolerate my bad behaviour because don't you realise I have been hurt, abused or abandoned." "How could I possibly have a healthy relationship with money, food or alcohol don't you understand the type of childhood I had." And on and on the list goes. The reason why you can't function in the world, why you can't be kind to people, can't hold down a job, get sober, get clean or be someone who makes a contribution to life is all as a result of those early woundings.

Instead of taking the path of the victim, what some of us

choose, is to take up the sword and shield of the warrior and step out into the world ready and willing to do battle with all. Here we strive to be the best at whatever we turn our attention to. We refuse to let our wounds yield any power over us. This however is a falsehood. As we walk the path of the warrior, we are still walking away from what hurt us and we are making damn sure that it doesn't get to hurt us again. And just to prove to the world that we are not damaged, we present the façade of achievement which ensures that the world knows what fine upstanding people we are. But the success and the achievement is hollow as it is built on rotting foundations, that will in time, be it years or decades, eventually crumble to the ground.

I know both of these archetypes very well as I have journeyed with them both. Each one presents its own protection mechanism which we use to save us from experiencing more pain, hurt and loneliness. But it takes huge energy to either wallow in victimhood or to be at war with the world. And one day when you least expect it your defences will break down.

My defences broke down when I was 29. I had at the time what is commonly called a breakdown. I have since come to think of it more as a breakthrough. I had a very well paid job in the television industry. I had returned to college at night, to study for a new degree. In addition I was also doing some occasional motivational speaking. And because, heaven forbid, I could sit still long enough to actually be with myself, I was also trying to sort out some serious financial problems my dad had gotten himself into, as well as having a relationship with my partner. Can you spot the archetype? I was the quintessential warrior, fighting to prove myself to the world, fighting to fix my family and fighting to show everyone that I could do it all with one hand tied behind my back and still have a very happy relationship. All the while I assumed that I appeared confident, competent and capable to the outside world.

I really believe that the universe knocks on your door to let you know that it is time to make some changes; that in fact all is not well in paradise. You may have a problem with your health, you may suffer from fatigue; you may find yourself irritable and anxious. In themselves they may be little things but they are designed to prompt you to sit up and look at your life, to consider that maybe it is time to start doing things differently, to evaluate what is going on for you.

For some people it works differently. You may notice or it may be pointed out to you that you are having more wine with your meals than usual; that you are less fun to be around; that your friends and family are worried about you. Whatever the signs are, only a lucky few of us catch them early. More often that not, however, we wait for the heart attack, for our partner to leave, or for some cataclysmic event to be catapulted into our lives before we will admit to ourselves things are not going 'quite right'.

I can remember that time in some ways very clearly. In some ways it is a complete blur, like a horrible dream that you have woken up from and don't really want to remember. I can also look back now and see with the clarity of hindsight when things started to slip. I found it hard to be motivated and interested in work. I hated Sunday evenings because it meant the next day was Monday again. Because I was on call 24/7, I flinched every time my cell phone rang in case it was the office. I was finding it increasingly hard to get out of bed in the mornings. I was tired and cranky all of the time and it was always someone else's fault. But I kept going.

Then one day I noticed a lump about the size of a large grape under my jaw bone. I went into panic and instead of going into work that morning I headed for the doctors office. After examining me, the doctor told me it was just a gland that was blocked and that there was no need to worry about it. I left her surgery and instead of being overcome with glee and relief that I was okay, I cried. I cried, and I kept on crying, I just couldn't stop, it was like someone opened the floodgates and nothing was going to stop that torrent of emotion from running through. Eventually when I composed myself, I called my office to let them know I wouldn't be in. I went home and yes you guessed it, I cried some more.

So was this the moment that changed my life? God no! I pulled myself together, went back to work and returned to studying. While still overseeing fixing my dads financial problems, I tried to convince myself that I had gotten a bad fright about the lump. I then tried to slip back into life as I knew it. But life wasn't the same as I knew it. I started to see it through different eyes. At the same time I battled with myself so that life would remain just the same. I wanted the job, the status, and the lifestyle. That was what I had worked so hard to achieve; that was my identity. But the rot had been exposed, albeit momentarily.

The moment that changed my life happened in the best tradition of fairy stories, 'on a day that was just like any other'. I was responsible for buying and scheduling programming for a satellite television channel that was broadcasting into the UK. We were by no means top of the pecking order when it came to channel status, but nevertheless contracts and schedules were negotiated like life itself and our salaries depended on it. I remember the day very clearly. I walked into the darkened control room with its rows of TV screens. I had to talk to the broadcast technician about a memo I had issued regarding a schedule change. This was a regular occurrence; live programming was a feature of our schedule and we would often have to change the running times of other shows to accommodate live programming. I spoke to the technician and I remember my attention being drawn to the large red power termination button in the corner of the room. It had always been there and was only ever to be used in an emergency.

In the live television industry, two of the more revered principles of broadcasting are, never have dead air, and never go to black. Dead air means that, for some reason there is nothing happening on the channel. There is a disruption in the broadcast. A presenter may forget their lines on a live show or there may be a technical hitch. Going to black is a similar principle. It means your signal is gone and the screen literally goes black as there is nothing being broadcast. Both are broadcasting faux pas. Not just because it is sloppy broadcasting but because in those moments when the programming stops there is a void. Two things can happen that you never want to happen in television. The first is that your viewer might, god forbid, switch to a different channel. The second is that the illusion is ruined. The viewer gets a sense that this is not a magical world. Instead it is regular people, doing a regular job, sometimes making regular mistakes.

So I looked at that button, and I thought: what would happen if I pressed it? What would be the worst scenario? People would complain. They wouldn't be able to see their soaps. But what if they couldn't see their soaps? They might actually do something instead like go out for a walk. And then ... the real clanger hit. "Oh my god, if I hit the button people might actually get on with their lives. In fact they might even have a better life not being glued to their TV screen. What I do, all this planning, stressing, programming, actually adds nothing to the quality of their lives. I actually make no positive contribution. If I stopped making a contribution most people probably wouldn't even notice. This thing that I do, this job, is actually of no value, and I am my job so ... Oh my god ... I am of no value".

That's when my tower of illusion started to tumble down. It was like someone kicked the wind right out of me. I felt limp, exhausted and empty. I completely understood how Dorothy must have felt when the curtain was pulled back to reveal the Wizard of Oz in his less than grandiose normalness of humanity. I lost my will. If all this was worthless, why do it? So I resigned. During the month that followed, as I worked out my notice, I dragged myself into the office most days. Some days it was just too much to bear. Each day I spiralled a little further down into a pit of darkness. But I was still the warrior. Did I open my heart to my colleagues, my friends and my family and explain what was happening to me? Of course not! In some twisted way I tried to maintain the façade that all was well in my world. It was time for a change, for something new. Of course, I reassured them I had a plan.

But there was no plan. All that there was, was my bed. That's what I crawled into and where I was determined never to crawl back out of.

A Recipe for Compost

Compost is natures nourishing fertilizer. Using it in your garden improves the quality and structure of the soil, giving plants a rich delicious foundation into which to send their roots. Compost is black gold; bringing valuable nutrients to your precious plants and vegetables.

The irony is that this rich organic substance is made from waste; kitchen waste, garden waste and manure; all the bits you don't want anymore or have no use for. They are provided with the right circumstances to break down, so that something much more valuable and nourishing can be created. Instead of trying to store our rot away where it will putrefy and contaminate everything in its environs, we need to take that raw matter and turn it into gold. This is the alchemical process.

The making of compost is like casting a delicious spell. In indigenous communities the medicine man or woman always works with the elements, earth, fire, water and air, to bring a sick member of the community back into balance and health. When making compost we work with all these elements to facilitate the creation of this dark rich hummus.

One of the most profound exercises I ever did was at a shamanic workshop many years ago. Everyone in the group had to pair off with someone else. You had to tell your partner all your secrets; all the things you had never told anyone. There was an awkward silence in the room when the exercise was explained.

The reason secrets are secrets are because you don't want to share your shame, embarrassment, guilt or humiliation with anyone else. Most people were slow to start, but once we did the floodgates opened, and as the backlog of secrets were released, in came the most amazing rush of freedom and lightness and relief. By sharing everything that we had kept hidden the energy was drained from our secrets. It was like a light had been shone into the darkness of your being only to discover that what was actually in there wasn't that bad. It just seemed bad because you were afraid to look at it and the fear built it up into this larger than life monster that you could never quite avoid or get away from.

To create something new, we must first honour and drain the energy from the old. We must let go of the parts of ourselves that no longer serve us, the parts of ourselves that are toxic and rotten. The following exercise is a process to transform your rot; to make compost for your soul; a rich fertile base where you can start your journey towards wholeness. When making compost all the elements are equally important as too much or too little of each affects the process. I ask you to take your time with the following exercise. You may wish to do it all in one sitting or you may wish to do it over several days. Go with what feels right for you. Every batch of compost is slightly different. Remember this is your journey, so you navigate the course.

Exercise – Making Compost

To make compost you will need the following:

A Compost Container

Treat yourself to a beautiful notebook or journal for doing the exercises, making notes and recording your thoughts. Have fun with the exercises, you may wish to use coloured pens. You may wish to doodle or draw on the pages. There may be pictures you like; that resonate with what you read in the following pages; that you wish to cut out and stick in. Sometimes you may be unable to find the word that represents your thought or feeling, so draw something instead. Remember the more varied the ingredients the better the compost.

For the following exercises, where you are required to write, please try and fill at least one full page. After a few lines you may feel like you have nothing left to say, but keep going. If you let your pen do the work and trust in the process you will often uncover the juiciest gems right after you think you have run out of steam. You may also find that you repeat yourself in some of the segments. That is okay too. The same vegetable peels often go into the compost heap day after day. It doesn't make the compost any less rich. Finally, you may notice that you contradict yourself on the same page. Again, that is perfect. We are trying to unleash everything that has been pushed down, and sometimes in pushing down the woundings we push our gifts down too. So now, if you are ready, let's make some compost.

Step 1 – Earth

Without vegetable peels, plant matter, or some good old fashioned manure, we have nothing to mulch to start the composting process.

- List out all the rot; all the toxic waste in your life, including all the limiting negative beliefs you have about yourself; hurtful things said to you by friends, family and work colleagues. Try to fill at least one full page. The more mulch you have, the more compost you make.
- List out as many of your woundings as you can, no matter how small or how old:

For example:

- I'm not good enough …
- I'm overweight …
- I'm an embarrassment to my family …
- I'm an alcoholic …
- I'm …

Step 2 – Air

The circulation of air through the mulch is an important component of compost. All the organisms that help break down the plant and vegetable matter need air to survive. Considering we do it automatically, most of us don't actually breathe properly. We take shallow breaths, which puts our body under physical strain. It also means that we become emotionally constipated. If you breathe, you access your feelings; you release pent up emotions, and you connect with your life source; the breath.

- Take ten minutes. Close your eyes. Relax your body. You can either sit up or lie down, but don't get so comfortable that you will fall asleep. Sleep is just resistance to the exercise.
- Start to breathe.
- Take long, slow, deliberate inhalations, followed by beautiful flowing exhalations.
- Feel that lovely breath washing in and out of your body like waves on the beach.
- Start to breathe into your feet, then on up into your calves, then your knees and so on, until you breathe into every part of your body.
- Notice the parts of your body that the breath finds it difficult to travel into.
- Notice any tightness or resistance in your body. Don't fight it, just notice it and keep breathing.
- When you have breathed into the crown of your head, take a few more delicious breaths down through the whole length of your body, and then open your eyes.
- Take a moment to notice how you are feeling. Do you feel any different than when you started the exercise? How does your body feel now?

Step 3 – Fire

The temperature of your compost heap is important in the decomposition process. If the heap is too cold the breakdown of matter won't occur. Heat is needed to destroy plant diseases and weed seeds that might be in the pile. Energetically, fire or heat is anger and passion. If passion is unlived or suppressed it surfaces as rage and angry outbursts. If we are to get the temperature of your compost pile just right, we need to find the balance between anger and passion.

- List out everything and everyone that you are angry with from your past all the way through to the present day, again trying to fill at least one full page.
- List out one more page of everything that you are passionate about. If there is nothing in your life that you are passionate about now write down things that you were passionate about as a child; eating ice cream, making mud pies, drawing pictures etc. Alternatively, write down things that you would like to be passionate about; your partner, your kids, your job, dancing a tango, making love, or walking barefoot on the beach.

Step 4 – Water

Organic waste needs moisture to decompose. However, if your compost heap is too wet, all you will create is a soggy mess. Water represents emotion. Many of us suppress our emotions. We keep them locked up in our inner Pandora's Box, so that we don't have to deal with something uncomfortable that is lurking inside. Sometimes however we don't even know what we are feeling. We don't have a name for it we just know that it doesn't feel good and that we don't want to feel it again.

- Take a few deep breaths and connect to your body.
- List all your feelings and your emotions positive and negative. If you don't know what you are feeling, draw an image, or use a colour that captures your emotion. Even numbness is a feeling. It is okay to feel contradictory emotions at the same time.

Step 5 – Compost Starter

Most gardeners introduce a compost starter into their heap. It contains micro organisms which help to initiate and speed up the composting process. The starter you need to instigate your healing process is called 'Willingness'. You have all the elements necessary to start composting the old you, but without willingness you will not succeed.

Many of us like, and in some cases love, the victim, the warrior, and the other plethora of archetypes that we have come to identify with. They are how we live our lives; they are the manifestation of our story. Who will we be and how will we survive without them? How will I get love if I can't tell you about how bad my life is or how hurt I am? How will I get validation if I have to let go of my desire to succeed?

Many of us say we want change, but in truth we don't. We may be suffering but the territory is very familiar, and we know how to navigate the terrain. It is not true that resistance is futile; most of us wallow in the pit of resistance because change is uncertain. We would rather put our energy into resisting change than taking a leap of faith into the unknown.

I think one of the greatest spiritual clichés is 'well it wasn't meant to be'. We can explain anything away with this seemingly enlightened phrase. You didn't get the parking space, the job, the date or the new car that you wanted because it wasn't meant to be. The fact of the matter is that maybe it was most definitely meant to be. The Universe was ready with open arms to present it to you, but the enormity of your resistance, for whatever reason, far outweighed the energy you were willing to manifest into creating or accepting something new. If you want to transform yourself from a barren wasteland to a tropical paradise you first need to be willing.

So before you proceed any further ask yourself, and answer honestly, otherwise you are only wasting your time.

* Are you willing to change?
* Are you willing to stoke the fire in your belly?
* Are you willing to find yourself, your colour and your passion?
* And are you willing to prepare the soil so that you can plant a rich and glorious garden?
* If you are willing take a pen, open a new fresh page in your journal and write:

* I _____ (insert your name) am Willing.

* You don't even have to know what you are 'willing' for. Once you are willing, the Universe will take care of the rest.
* Gardeners are experts in noticing; noticing the weather, noticing when the first buds start to appear, noticing if their plants need food or protection from the elements. Making your own compost is an exercise in noticing. There is no right or wrong

way to do it. Simply notice what memories, feelings and experiences come up to the surface ready to be digested and transformed into something new. Gardeners don't suffer from guilt. They understand the cycles of nature, and that sometimes something has to die for something new to be created. Don't feel guilty about your lists. If you feel guilt, resistance, discomfort etc. write it down on your compostable materials list. Don't hold back. The more you write the richer and more bountiful your compost will be.

Sowing the Seeds

M^y bed offered no comfort. It was not the safe haven I had hoped for. It was instead more like a holding area. I was too tired and too exhausted to get out of it, but each waking moment in it was torturous. I couldn't keep my 'bad dreams file' closed anymore. It haunted me. The more I tried to fight it the more it screamed to be seen and heard. I floundered around in the quagmire, being forced to look at myself at every turn. No matter how hard I tried to hide from it, the horrible realisation that kept stalking me was that I was miserable. Behind the disguise of the bubbly, ever helpful media executive was a miserable, sad and lonely soul.

Yet the final blow was still to come. I had worked so hard in my job. I had been working so hard to help my dad out of the hole he had dug himself into. I was hurting so bad and feeling so lost, and yet no one rang to see how I was or how I was doing. There were no kind words from any of the people I had worried and stressed over. I felt abandoned and used. Looking back now I can see that they had no idea what was going on, so why would they ring or call? My partner was the only one I really saw or spoke to. He didn't understand what was going on any more than I did, but he loved and supported me, and tried to be patient.

The more I dwelt on my inadequacies and hurts, the more I cried, trying to purge myself of the insurmount-able pain that dwelled within. Many nights I prayed to die just so the pain would stop. Each morning before I would open my eyes, there was a moment where I would optimistically check to see if perhaps my prayer had been granted. This momentary hope would be replaced by the stark realisation that I had indeed made it through another agonising night.

As it seemed that God wasn't going to let me die, and as I actually hadn't the gumption to do anything about it myself, I decided that I had to do something to help alleviate the pain. I decided to go to a counsellor, which was a huge step for me. In Ireland, unlike America, people did not mention, except in hushed tones to someone you knew very well (only after they had sworn on the life of their nearest and dearest never to tell another living soul) that you were in fact seeing 'a shrink'. I remember watching American movies and soap operas when I was younger and looking at people as they lay on their psychotherapists couch wondering do they not have any friends they could talk to. The whole thing seemed strange and unnecessary to me; the irony of it being that I had some beautiful friends but I was damned if I was going to share my woes with them.

Nobody talked about seeing a therapist. As I didn't want to ask where I might find one, in case it might attract attention, I applied the fail safe method and consulted the all knowing encyclopaedia of wisdom that is The Yellow Pages. It actually seems funny now, but at the time I was so desperate and so scared. I can't remember if I looked up Counselling, Psychotherapy or Crazy Woman in Need of Help, but the phone book fell open with the details of a counselling practice that had a dove in their logo. I got nervous and closed the phone book, but something inside me willed me on. I opened it again 'randomly' and the same dove logo magically appeared in front of me. Very slowly, and nervously, I dialled, almost hoping that no one would answer. In what seemed like seconds, a very professional person on the other end of the phone, (who seemed perfectly at ease with the fact that people would call a therapists office) had made an appointment for me to see Pauline.

Pauline was like a breath of fresh air. She was middle aged, very elegant, gentle features and so very kind. She looked like someone's mum, and at the same time exuded professionalism and wisdom. She asked me why had I come, and it all tumbled out. Nothing seemed to faze her; she didn't seem to think that I was going mad. She seemed very comfortable with the blubbering wreck of a woman that was sitting across from her.

And so this is how our journey together began. Once a week I would drive to see her. Gently and patiently she would help me drain the energy from the pain I had been carrying. It was like someone had opened the nozzle on a pressure cooker. At last the steam could find its way out.

In time I finally confided in a friend of mine as to what was going on. I remember being overcome by her love, her concern, and her complete lack of judgement. She proceeded to make an appointment for me to see a spiritual reader. Her hope was that I might get some guidance or understanding of the situation. I didn't know anything about spiritual readings but something about it just felt right. For some strange reason, I remember exactly what I was wearing that day, black knee high boots, a dark green skirt and a green turtle neck sweater. I felt like I had to make a good impression, but it was a waste of time.

The lady who did the reading had a lovely warm smile. She didn't look at what I was wearing. Instead, she looked right into my soul. It was an amazing experience. She explained what was happening to me, and how I could help the healing process. Of course I cried. I don't think a day went by without tears, but I came away with the feeling that everything was going to be okay. I remember the last thing she said to me was, "You are emotional enough, so it might be better if you don't wear green for a while. Green is the colour of your heart chakra and it doesn't need any extra stimulation right now". She *had* noticed what I was wearing, but not for the reasons I had expected.

I think we all reach for something when we are desperate. No matter how bad I felt, the one thing I was determined not to reach for was alcohol. Alcoholism ran too deeply in my family, and as much as I didn't want to feel my pain, I knew if I tried to numb it with alcohol I would be on the losing side of a much bigger battle.

Instead, I turned to God and every one of his angels. I always had a strong belief in God; not so much in the Irish Catholic God, but in the sense that there was a higher power. Once I got over the fact that he wasn't going to let me die, I prayed for help; help to feel better in myself, help to stop crying, help that the exhaustion would pass. The list went on and on.

Amazing things started to happen. Wonderful people

came into my life. They did indeed help me, listen to ￼
and guide me through. My partner was amazing. He pai￼
the bills and looked after the house when I couldn't.

One night over dinner, I remember turning to him
and telling this beautiful man who had been so kind and
loving to me, that I didn't think I loved him. I saw the
pain and hurt those words inflicted. He was upset and
angry. The truth I came to learn later was the person
that I didn't love was myself. I think part of me wanted
to drive him away; to prove to myself what a horrible
person I was and how bad things were in my life. But
he was loving and stubborn, and despite my best efforts,
he stayed and kept loving me. In time things started to
change. I started to have more energy. The days became
brighter, and it felt at last like I was beginning to leave
the darkness behind.

I started to take some workshops. Initially, they
were one day workshops, using animal imagery to help
you heal. They were powerful in their simplicity. They
helped me see past my hurt. I learned about the spiritual
journey; how we are here to learn life lessons, clear our
karma and grow as spiritual beings. I never questioned
any of it. Not in a gullible 'I believe everything you are
telling me' sort of way, but I never doubted that I was
a spiritual being having a physical experience. It just felt
right to me. It was like something in my soul knew it to
be true.

ious amount during that time. I read

gels, Shamanism, healing, and the

Any book or tape that I was guided

ously. Some of the material was new

challenging, but more often than not it was like remembering something I had long since forgotten. I could see all the people and events in my life like a jigsaw puzzle; all fitting together; all part of something greater that I didn't totally understand. Yet it all felt so perfectly right. Some friends that I spoke to at that time thought it was all mumbo jumbo; something that I was latching onto to make me feel better, but I knew it wasn't. I knew there was something inside me pulling me forward. It was like an inner compass, and I began to realise that the reason I had broken down, or broken through, was that I was so dramatically off course.

As well as going to see Pauline for counselling, I also experimented with just about every alternative therapy available at the time; body massage, reflexology, colour therapy, Reiki, aura reading, aura therapy, crystal therapy, and whatever else I could find. Some of it didn't do anything for me, some of it just helped me to relax and get some well needed sleep, but some of it really seemed to make a difference. Some sessions helped me to let go of the pain and the darkness and take another baby step towards the light.

I discovered, to my amazement, that I wasn't on my own.

I wasn't the only one who was lost or depressed or broken. There were lots of people out there, all with their own story, trying to hang on for dear life. Somehow there was great comfort in hearing about other people's struggles. Not because I wanted to see them in pain. I knew what pain felt like and didn't wish it on anyone else. What it did mean in some weird way was that I was normal. It was normal to be upset, normal not to be able to keep it all together, normal to be going to a counsellor and normal to be looking for help. God, what a relief!

Sowing seeds in a garden is a magical experience. Like poppies, some seeds are tiny and almost microscopic. Some, like sunflowers, are much more robust. The one thing they have in common, however, is that they are often generic and lack lustre. They are dry and hard and give no indication of the potential that dwells inside. But when you place them into the belly of the earth, and present them with the right conditions, moisture, heat and time, they eventually reach upwards. They stretch out into the light to unveil their beauty and magnificence.

As your new seedlings emerge into the world, you must look after them, remove any weeds that may choke them or drain valuable nutrients from them and feed them so that they can become strong and hardy to the elements. It is the same for people. If we provide ourselves with the right conditions, and allow ourselves the gift of time, we too will blossom.

I remember the day I found myself. There was a cupboard under the stairs in the front hallway of my house. I used to keep lots of kitchen stuff in it; pots, pans and baking tins. The hall was painted red, and when the sun shone in through the glass on either side of the front door, it lit up the space and filled it with a radiant amber glow. One afternoon, the sun was shining into the hall. I opened the door of the cupboard to get something out. While one hand was still on the door handle, I turned and reached my other hand into the cupboard, and it was like something went click in my body. It was almost like watching someone do a Rubik's cube.

When you start out with a Rubik's cube it's all jumbled. Finally there is that one final twist when it all comes together. When I felt that internal click I knew in an instant that I was back together. I felt like me again; an old me that I had long since forgotten. I was so very glad that she was back.

I don't know how long I stood there for, with one hand on the handle, and with one hand reaching into the cupboard. I was afraid if I moved the feeling would go away. But I knew I couldn't stay like this forever. At some point my partner would come home and wonder who this woman was, frozen, like a statue in the hallway.

Ever so slowly, I started to move. I started to bring my outstretched arm back towards my body. As I moved, I told myself that if, at any point, this feeling started to slip away, I would stop. But the feeling didn't go away. As I brought my arms to my sides, I started to breathe this feeling deep into my body. That is where it stayed. It was strong and tangible and very familiar. After all these months of being lost, I had eventually found my way home.

From Caterpillar to Butterfly

The healing journey is an inner journey. We can reach out and ask for help, but ultimately we have to go within and address the woundings that live inside. Many of us choose suffering over healing. We cram our systems with food, alcohol, narcotics and endless distractions to push down the rot so that we don't have to deal with it. I know many people who talk a good talk; talk about personal healing; finish every sentence with "love and light", or "God bless you", but don't actually engage in their own healing process. If you do go within, however, there is beauty ready to be made manifest.

When the caterpillar retreats into its cocoon, it does

not do so because it knows it will emerge as a beautiful butterfly. It does so because there is an instinctual calling to retreat and weave its delicate blanket. The metamorphosis is difficult, while in the cocoon the caterpillar is vulnerable and exposed. Still it persists until it emerges transformed.

I am going to invite you to participate in a metamorphic process. I appreciate some of you might think this exercise is difficult and is somewhat premature, as we have only just begun our journey together. My mission is to take you on a journey to your inner garden; to the deep rich moist feminine that lives within. To do that, we need to let go of what binds us to the past.

Exercise – Time Line

• For a moment imagine your life as a time line. In your minds eye place a mark on that time line at each point where you were wounded. Imagine one chord for each wounding coming from your heart, through your back, and attaching itself to that place in time where you were hurt. It's almost like being an octopus and your tentacles are reaching behind you, clasping tightly to those frozen moments in time. Try and take one step forward and see what it feels like.

I can guarantee that for most of you, taking that step forward is next to impossible, as you are so intensely chorded to the past, and that's okay. But if you want to move forward we need to remove the chords. Some healing modalities would ask you to cut or sever the chords. However, in my experience, if you cut the chords in the absence of love, all you are left with is raw wounds either side of the cut. The wounds will continue to fester over time.

One of the most transformative healing energies is the energy of forgiveness. By forgiving ourselves and others, we smooth cooling balm on our throbbing wounds and allow those chords to dissolve. Forgiveness frees us from the past, and, as we forgive, we let go of the toxic energy that we hold in our bodies, in our minds, and in our energy field.

For the following exercise it might be helpful to remember that:

You are a Divine Being. You are created in the image and likeness of the Divine Mother Father God, and so therefore you are perfection. You incarnated into this world to learn and to grow, based on experiences that are not available to you if you reside in the energetic plane. If you are Divine, and you reside in the Divine, (call it heaven, nirvana, or whatever corresponds with your spiritual belief) you cannot learn the lessons of trust, forgiveness, compassion etc. because you vibrate to the frequency of pure love.

In love there is only love. Any emotion or energy

of a lower vibration (hate or fear) cannot exist in the presence of love. When I worked as a shamanic healer, I used to work with clients on clearing past lives, curses, old woundings etc. that were still affecting them. What I learned was that, instead of focusing on the past, if you facilitate the client in aligning to love, everything else disappeared. The heavy binding energy of the past could not coexist in the presence of love.

Having a physical body is a huge blessing. It means that you get to acquire a whole array of knowledge and teachings that would otherwise not be available to you.

I know I personally questioned the fact that, if I came from love, why did I not remain as love, instead of coming down to this earthly plane to get hurt? There were many times when I turned to God and asked to renegotiate my soul contract, because all this learning wasn't a whole lot of fun. It is the nature of every species to evolve, and through the gift of incarnation, our species gets to progress. Many will say that our species, for all its technological advances, has not progressed; that there is more hate and violence in the world, and that we are poisoning our planet. This is not true.

We are in the University of Life, and we are studying at master's level. The lessons presented to us at this time are some of the greatest in the history of our species. We are being asked to love globally; to reach out across neighbourhoods, countries, and our planet, to sow the seeds of love in the places where fear and hate runs deep.

It is easy to love your pet, or your child. It is much more difficult to love someone whose thoughts and actions are so diametrically opposed to yours. That is the real journey. That is what will really exercise your spiritual muscles. If you are a republican, think about loving the democrats; not just tolerating them, but loving them. If you are a Christian, think about loving a Jew or a Muslim. If you are a rape victim, think about loving your attacker. If you are a rapist, think about loving the person you attacked. This is the meaning of mastery.

Forgiveness does not mean that you sweep what happened under the carpet. It means that you acknowledge the event. Then you see it for what it is; an opportunity to grow, to learn, and to heal. If you were whole and complete, you would not need the lesson to grow. If the person who facilitated the lesson with you was whole and complete, the lesson could not have happened. The situation, even at the time it appeared to cause a wounding, was a wonderful orchestration by the Universe. Two souls were brought together to facilitate each other on their healing path.

I realise this is quite a leap of faith for some of you. And I am not asking you to fake it until you make it. What I am asking you is; are you willing to let go of those chords that are binding you so tightly to the past? If you try the following exercise and you don't feel any different afterwards, that is fine. But if you have taken this book off the shelf and started to read it, there is something inside you that is longing for change. Something inside you is trying to realign your inner compass, and be available to live life, as opposed to lingering in the woundings of the past. What I am asking you is; are you ready to stop being the caterpillar and embrace the metamorphosis and transform?

The reason we speak the following words out loud is that there is an energy to speech. It comes from your fifth chakra which is located in your throat and which contains the energy of will. By speaking out loud you are affirming your willingness to allow the energy of forgiveness to flow into each situation. Speaking also triggers neurotransmitters in your brain which help your mind to rewire what it 'thought' about the situation. In doing so, they change your perception of the events. It doesn't mean that the event didn't happen, but you can change your perception from one of hurt or wounding to one of love and learning. Speaking out loud also allows you to be witnessed. In lighting a candle you are symbolically doing this exercise in the presence of Spirit, you will be allowing Spirit to both witness and facilitate your healing.

I would recommend that you do this exercise in stages; breaking it up into manageable chunks. You can then give each segment the necessary time and attention.

If emotions, words or images come up for you during the exercise remember to keep breathing and make a note of them in your journal. Some of the situations may require you to return to them several times before the energy is clear. That's okay. This is a work in progress, but it is also symbolises that you are taking responsibility for your healing, and taking a giant step away from the energy of victimhood.

Each time you complete part of this exercise please be gentle with yourself. You may wish to curl up in a nice blanket and listen to some gentle music. You may wish to spend time in your garden, or in nature. Treat yourself to a massage or something that nurtures you.

When the caterpillar emerges from her cocoon she is initially vulnerable. There is a short period where her wings must dry, and where she must get used to her new body, before she can take flight and share her radiance with the world. You are that butterfly. Tread gently, my love.

Exercise – Finding Forgiveness in our Compost.

For the following exercise you will need:

- A mirror that you can see your face in
- A lighted candle
- Your notebook and pen

The candle represents Divine Spirit, which will transmute any heavy energy as you work through the following exercise. The Divine Spirit also represents love. You are doing this exercise in the presence of pure, unconditional love. Open your notebook where you listed out the items you wished to compost.

Earth
....

A lot of our rot is based on belief systems that no longer serve us.

- For every item you have written on your earth list, say out loud, while looking into the mirror;
- I forgive myself for thinking that …
- I forgive myself for thinking that I'm not good enough …
- I forgive myself for being overweight …
- I forgive myself for thinking that I am an embarrassment to my family …
- I forgive myself for allowing myself to get hurt …

For the items that you have written that include another person, close your eyes, take a breath, call up an image of that person, and say:

- I forgive _____ for …

- I forgive my dad for saying I was stupid …
- I forgive my teacher for saying that I would never amount to anything …
- I forgive my boss for …

Air

When you did the first Air exercise you noticed if there was any tension, resistance or restriction in your body. It is now time to revisit your body and release that stagnant energy.

- Breathe deeply and connect with your breath.
- Follow the breath into your body and once again become aware of any tension, pain, restriction etc.
- On the exhale, gently say: 'I forgive myself for holding tension in my neck, chest, belly etc.'
- Keep repeating the exercise until you feel that the majority of the tension has been released from your body.

Fire

When you are ready you can move on to the list you have for Fire.

Repeat the forgiveness process for everything you feel angry about.

- I forgive myself for feeling angry at …
- You do not do this exercise for the items that you are passionate about. If, however, you want to feel passionate about something you are disconnected from; e.g. I want to feel passionate about making love, your job etc. you can say;
- I forgive myself for not feeling passionate about making love.
- I forgive myself for not feeling passionate about my job.
- In doing so, you help to clear any blockages that are stopping you from having passion in your life.

Water

It is important to honour the spectrum of emotions that you can feel. Now repeat the exercise for your Water list.

- Use only the emotions that have a negative charge.
- For example, if you have written down, "I feel loved", and have also written "I feel unloved" (remember, it's fine to have a contradiction; you could feel unloved by a family member but loved by a friend), you only have to forgive the negative emotion.
- I forgive myself for feeling unloved by …
- I forgive myself for feeling sad about …
- I forgive myself for being grumpy with …

And Finally …

....

- Place in front of you all the items you are passionate about from your Fire list. For each item you are passionate about, say into the mirror;
- I honour my passion for …
- Take out your Water list, and for any positive emotions that you have written, say into the mirror;
- I honour that I feel …

No matter what our life experiences have been, in the eyes of God, we are perfection. Finally, take three deep breaths, look into the mirror and repeat several times;

- I love and embrace all parts of myself.
- I am Woman.
- I am a rich evolving tapestry.
- I am planting a new garden.
- I have made rich compost for my seeds.
- And so it is.

Now rest and drink some water. You have released lots of old energy. Be gentle with yourself and allow your body and your soul to recalibrate and settle.

When the Seed Cracks

I fiercely protected my new found self. I was afraid that I would exhaust the supply of this new energy that was coming into my life. I was afraid after working so hard to find it, that it might go away if I didn't look after it. But the energy wasn't finite. I needed to nurture it, and respect it, but it wasn't going anywhere. It was here to stay, and day by day it, and I, grew stronger and stronger.

After working with Pauline for several months I felt our work was complete. It was not that everything in my life was sorted, however she had helped me release so much of the emotional backlog. I felt that I was equipped with a good set of tools that I could use in life, and I knew if the road became rocky again that I could return to her. I also felt that I had to find my own way. I didn't want to become dependent on her. I needed to apply the wisdom and skills that I had learned from my time with her to my life. I needed to see if I could make it on my own.

As time passed, my health improved and I grew in confidence. I decided to participate in a residential work-shop, which was being run at the Burren Holistic Centre in the west of Ireland, by the Spiritual Reader that I had met so many months before. The Burren Centre is an amazing place. The gardens of the centre slope down to meet the grey limestone plateau of the Burren, a lunar landscape which then sweeps up to form the rolling peak, Mullagh More, one of the sacred mountains of the west.

The Burren Centre was run by Bridin Twist, a woman who terrified me when I first met her. Not because she was particularly scary, but because, despite your best efforts to present a brave face to the world, you felt like she could see into the depths of your heart. You felt like she knew your secrets.

Bridin personified the title 'Wise Woman of the West'. She was an amazing cook, and nourished everyone that came to stay in her centre with her food and her words. She also had the wickedest, filthiest, most contagious laugh I have ever heard. Soon after arrival you would be sitting in her cosy kitchen with a cup of tea in one hand, a piece of cake in the other and you would start to feel as if this was your home. Sadly Bridin has now left this world, but so much of her spirit and what she taught me lives on in my heart.

The theme of this workshop was personal healing and accessing your intuition. I think part of me thought it would be a nice weekend away; lovely scenery, good food, and the company of people who were in a similar situation in life. I couldn't have been more wrong. There are certain pivotal moments in our life. For me this workshop was one of them.

During one of the exercises, the image of a tall slim man with mousey brown shoulder length hair, and a tight clipped beard, appeared to me. I started to dialogue with him, as we had been shown how to by the facilitator. He explained to me that his name was Joseph. He was a spirit guide and he was here to help me read. I didn't understand what this meant so I questioned him further. He said I was a reader, and he explained that he was here to help me do psychic readings for people.

I went into a complete flip. I wasn't a reader, nor did I want to be one. I had spent the best part of my life feeling different everyone from else, and I didn't want to add to the sense of isolation or eccentricity that I sometimes felt about myself. No matter what way you looked at it calling yourself a psychic definitely veered on the eccentric side. I tried to imagine going home to my parents and saying; "Hi mam. Hi dad. Guess what, I'm a psychic now." My stomach knotted. I thanked him very much, and said; "Thank you, but no thank you."

Joseph must have been a Taurean in a past life, because as stubborn as I thought I was, he outmatched me every time. He kept turning up all weekend. Whenever we were given an exercise or a meditation, he was there. I kept ignoring him, convinced that he would get bored, and that he would eventually go away. On the last day of the workshop our facilitator said she was going to divide us up into groups of two or three, and that we were going to read for each other.

I couldn't believe it. The one thing I really didn't want to do in the whole world loomed in front of me. You could say; "Why didn't I just decide not to do the exercise", but you forget, I was a warrior. I may not have wanted to do it, but losing face, or failing at a task, is not an option if you hold the warrior archetype. I gathered my sword and my shield and joined the two ladies to whom I had been assigned. As often happens in these situations, once you engage in the energy, it is not nearly as horrendous as you imagined. I sat with the two women, and we had a nice time as we progressed through the exercise. When it was my turn to read, Joseph told me word for word what I was to say. After the initial fear and resistance it felt so completely natural and easy.

As the workshop continued, I knew I had to make a choice. Joseph was unrelenting. I knew on some deep level that, even though the human part of me was screaming not to have anything to do with this psychic nonsense, another part of me wanted to be available to God. At the time, I didn't fully understand what that meant or how it would work. As the workshop came to an end I was consumed with the desire to release the words that were now stuck in my throat. I knew that saying them was not enough. I had to say them out loud, and be witnessed. I walked across the room to one of the women, with whom I had worked with earlier that day and said to her; "I will do it." I don't know if she had a clue what I was talking about, but she held me, looked into my eyes and said; "I know you will." In that instant I knew I would, and then together we cried.

During the months of sowing my seeds in the hope of finding myself I never imagined that when the seed pod cracked the flower that would emerge would have psychic capabilities. I really believe that Spirit only gives us the information that we can handle at any point in time. If we are told too much we would be overwhelmed by the task ahead. Instead we are provided with stepping stones that lead us gently to our new destination.

Being a psychic was definitely never one of the boxes I ticked on my list of career choices. On reflection I can see that some of the signs were always there. I was always incredibly sensitive. I felt peoples joy and sadness. I was able to read between the lines of the words they spoke. My mother is also incredibly intuitive. When we were growing up she would often say things about our family or neighbours that we would dismiss as fanciful only to find out later that she was right. But to think that I was a psychic felt uncomfortable.

I had affirmed my willingness to God and I prayed for guidance, but I didn't know how this gift worked or what I was supposed to do with it. One evening a friend of mine whose dad had recently passed away called over. She was experiencing the rawness of the hurt and the pain that his loss had brought. As we were talking, Joseph appeared. While I was talking to my friend, he started talking to me. He said, "If you read for her it will help". I was having none of it.

We had been friends since we were kids. We hung out together, grew up together, and chased boys together. There was no way I was going to tell her that her life long friend was now a psychic. But Joseph kept persisting. He insisted that I read for her. Round and around it went until I felt my head was going to explode. Out of sheer frustration I telepathically said to him, "ALRIGHT!" I don't remember the exact words I used, but it went along the lines of, "I hope you don't find this weird, but if you like I could read for you and it might help".

Without batting an eyelid (or if she did I didn't notice) she said "Yes".

With Josephs help I started to read. He would tell me what I needed to say and I would repeat it. At one point her dad appeared in front of me and spoke to her through me. This was my first ever 'proper' reading. It lasted for over two hours, and to this day it remains one of the most beautiful readings I have ever done. Thankfully we have remained very good friends.

My second reading was an equally memorable experience. I was at a party with people that I used to work with. Joseph drew my attention to a woman that I briefly knew. He was adamant that I should approach her and offer to read for her. I was mortified. I barely knew her. Whenever I looked in her direction she was in the company of friends. It felt like a dream, but before I knew it I was standing beside her, explaining myself and what I did. She was delighted that I had approached her. She arranged to call me during the week to make an appointment. That's how it all started. One person told another person, and then people started to come to my house for readings.

Joseph tutored me in how to read. At first, it was a tough apprenticeship. It was like a three way conversation. The client would ask me a question. Joseph would speak to me. Then I would repeat what he said, word for word, to the client. His mantra was, "Do not under any circumstances change my words or deliver them differently in an attempt to make the client feel better". This was a valuable teaching. Sometimes I wouldn't understand what he said, but the client would. Sometimes the words he used had special significance for the client, and sometimes the message was blunt. If the message was blunt, my natural reaction would be to candy coat it, but he would not allow that. As I came to understand, he sometimes had to be blunt with clients to get the seriousness of what he was saying across.

He taught me how to open and close 'sacred space', so that the energy (both where I was working and between the client and I) would be clear. He helped me to see a clients energy body (their aura and chakras) when they sat across from me. He taught me how to see the story behind the fracture or discoloration in their energy field, and present the client with a template for healing. The most important thing he taught me was how to trust; how to trust him, my own intuition, and ultimately how to trust in God. As I sat across from clients I learned to trust Joseph's guidance. Once I pushed my own self doubt, fears and feelings of inadequacy out of the way I could become a channel for the Divine.

In time it stopped being a three way conversation. Once I opened sacred space, it was like Joseph and I merged, but I always remained aware, of which voice was mine and which was his.

I soon realised that I would have to stop inviting people over to my house. I had issues about charging people for readings. I felt like I was a novice. It was a bit cheeky to expect a fee, so their session would last for hours. Afterwards I would make them tea to the point where they were nearly taking up residence in my home. I also had two beautiful dogs. Every time a spirit would arrive to talk to a client the dogs would sense it and become irritated. I felt that I needed to reclaim my home, and adopt a more professional approach to the work I was doing.

While having a massage one Friday, I mentioned to the masseuse that I needed to find somewhere to work. She suggested that I speak to the woman who ran 'The Haven,' one of the centres she worked in. Before I knew it, I had agreed to work as an 'intuitive' every Saturday in the Haven.

Secretly, I doubted my abilities. I thought that if I booked a room for which I was now paying rent and if no one turned up, I could say to God, "Well I committed; I did what you asked me and it didn't work. Thanks all the same but I'm going back to building a 'normal' life now."

What I hadn't figured on, but obviously God had, was Enid. Enid ran The Haven. She was a walking talking PR machine for therapists. If she believed in you, even if you didn't believe in yourself, she made sure everyone knew about you. In the blink of an eye my Saturdays were booked out. Because I was paying rent, and I was now taking appointments, I had to refine my craft.

I learned to be less sloppy in my approach, to read more concisely and to spend less time reaffirming what Joseph was saying. This, I also learned, took a lot less energy. When I let Divine guidance flow through me I felt less drained. I came to see that what I had considered a burden was blossoming into a beautiful gift.

The Haven was a beautiful place to work. It was an old converted cottage, situated in a picturesque village beside the sea. In the summertime it buzzed with holidaymakers and locals enjoying the sunshine and the sights. What made The Haven even more special were the women who worked there. From the minute I started, I was made welcome. It was like being pulled into the bosom of a loving family.

I have worked in a lot of places and it is very rare to work in a place where everyone likes each other. Sometime there are personality clashes, or people fall out over petty things. That never happened here. Though we were different ages, from different backgrounds, we laughed together, cried together and grew together. We supported each other, and referred clients to each other. Most importantly, we never judged each other. No matter what was going on in your life, you got an honest opinion (several honest, often different, opinions, actually). Whatever help you needed was offered gladly and lovingly.

Working there was a huge learning experience for me on many different levels. I learned to hone my craft, and work with Joseph. Joseph continually taught me about Spirit and the Spiritual journey. I saw that, if I didn't process my own issues, the issues would then present themselves in my clients. I became very conscious and diligent about processing my issues, and working from a place of integrity.

One of the biggest life lessons I learned at The Haven was about sharing. I used to think I was a private person. Really I was just my mother's daughter. The habit of not talking about my business, or airing my laundry in public, had been instilled in me from childhood. In the early days of working with these women I was dumb-struck by the fact that they talked about everything. They talked about their families, their friends, their kids, their feelings and their sex lives.

Occasionally, in the early days, I felt like I was in an episode of 'Sex and the City'. It made me feel uncomfortable and awkward. Over time, as I let my defences down and engaged with these fantastic women, I adored the freedom and release that sharing brought. We didn't share so that someone else could fix our problems. We shared just to share. In the sharing we learned about ourselves: our thoughts and emotions. We learned about what made us laugh and cry. And we grew ...

I learned that, when we don't keep things bottled inside, there is an opportunity to explore how we really feel. Sometimes, something that seems to carry such emotional weight for us, once shared, seems lighter and less significant.

As awkward as this was for me to begin with, I really started to look forward to our chats. In time I came to realise that there was a part of me that had actually been longing for this. I didn't want to be locked up inside myself; isolated and alone. I wanted to share. Between us we didn't have all the answers, but we did have a wealth of experience from which to draw on. The more I shared, the freer I felt within myself. The Haven had become my haven; a sanctuary for my soul.

New Growth

There is a story of remembering and it goes something like this ...

Once upon a time when the world was young, back at the beginning of time, women gathered in circle, in what came to be known as the Red Tent. This was no ordinary tent; no ordinary place. It was a mystical connection to the Divine; to Mother Earth; to all that is, all that was, and all that had yet to come. This was a sacred site, and yet its location was not fixed or permanent. In truth, the Red Tent lived within, but was expressed without.

The Red Tent was an answer to a calling; something deep that lived within. It called to the women, but they did not know from where. The calling had been in them since birth. It came to them in dreamtime. And when they were ripe with blood, they would be called to sit in circle as one.

No one knew who started the first Red Tent. No one knew who explained what was to happen at each gathering. And yet everyone knew. Instinctively they knew when it was time to go; to gather and to be heard; to teach, to share and to show the skills they had learnt. Among the Navaho they say it was Spider Woman who taught the women. Some say it was Mother Mary. Some say it was the Earth herself. It does not matter. All that matters now is that you remember. Remember your calling to the Red Tent.

During the month when each woman in the tribe was ripe with blood, they would withdraw from the men folk. They would be relieved from their duties and withdraw to the safe haven of the Red Tent. Together they would sit and they would bleed. The rich ripe flow of menstrual blood would be gathered in straw or cotton, and kept safely for the three days while they rested in the Red Tent. Some of the blood would be returned to Mother Earth, the universal mother who had birthed all her children. She would be honoured with the blood of their being, for the gift of life and death. Some of the blood would be mixed with water, and this pure nourishment used to feed the crops so that they would grow tall and bear fruit. Some would be ground to powder and paste, and used in healing remedies for the land, the tribe and the animals. All was done with complete reverence, humility and love.

The women watched their men folk go to hunt and they knew the dangers it brought. Many a strong warrior had bled to death after being pierced by the fangs of a beast. And yet the women bled, month after month, until it was no longer their time. They emerged refreshed, renewed and alive. They knew the power of the blood. They knew the wisdom that could be attained by the blood mysteries, and so they honoured. They honoured each other, the earth and the men, for without men there would be no women, and they honoured the sacredness and unity of all as one.

As they sat in circle they shared much. Their shared their hopes, their dreams and their pain. Their shared the news that their men folk had brought from far off lands. They shared their healing. They shared the omens that had come to them in dreamtime; how to live, love and protect their tribe. They shared the teachings of the healing herbs. There were herbs for good health, herbs to help you die peacefully, herbs to help you give birth and herbs to honour the ancestors. For every herb there was a story, and for the herb to be used the story had to be told.

Everyone knew the stories but in the telling they

remembered. They remembered who they were, where they had come from and where they had yet to go. They shared birthing stories so the new mothers could ready themselves. They shared dying stories so the elders could prepare themselves to leave. And when young women came of age, and were initiated into the red tent they told the story of the first 'Blood' and the honour of allowing the wisdom of 'Woman' to flow through them so that they could connect with the earth.

This is the story of the blood mysteries. For many it has been forgotten. For some it still lives within. Open the door to your inner Red Tent, and allow yourself to remember. Remember the spirit of who you are.

I really believe that huge healing comes from sharing our stories. You realise that you are 'not the only one'. Sharing collapses the secret prison into which we cast ourselves when we carry shame or guilt, or feelings of inadequacy. The key to sharing, however, is to open the drapes and let the light come right in. Once you share your story the healing follows. Allow the laughter, the tears and the new found wisdom to replace the hurt, and then be prepared to let go.

You must be willing to let go of your story so that it becomes just that, a story. It no longer binds you. Many of us love our stories and we are reluctant to relinquish them. For without them, who are we? The truth is that you are not your story. You are much more, and yet much less. You are Divine creation made manifest. This is everything and it is nothing. If you realise you are Divine creation you don't need to be your woundings or your story. You are perfect just as you are.

I remember attending a shamanic workshop at one time and being quite upset that no one was interested in my story. What they were interested in was how to stop your story from shaping your life. During that workshop I realised how much energy I had invested in my story. Whether I shared it or not, it had become my identity. Each wound was a marking like stripes on a tiger. If I didn't have my stripes what would distinguish me from the other tigers?

What I have learned is that the more we relinquish our wounds the more we allow our inner light to shine. The experience of our wounds allows this inner flame to burn brighter, because if we clear the wounding we become more acutely aware of our sense of self. Many spiritual texts tell us that we have chosen our wounds so that we can heal, both for ourselves and for our families. In doing so, we evolve as spiritual beings, and we clear the karma of the past. I can honestly tell you that there were times when knowing this brought me absolutely no comfort. I was hurting and I didn't care about spiritual journeys or evolving.

Looking back I can see now how each difficult situation I have encountered has brought me to a deeper understanding of myself. Each situation has brought another glorious soul into my life that has helped me move forward on the stepping stones of life. If you see tigers in the wild, or even in the zoo, you will probably not remember their individual stripes. But you will remember their gait, their prowess, their essence. This is why we must let go of our stories, so that we can let our essence be free. It is our essence (not our woundings) that improves our lives, and ultimately brings change to the world.

I have gone to counselling at different times in my life and I have found it very helpful. It can be a wonderful process, but it can also be a wonderful trap. I do not say this lightly. Counselling or psychotherapy is a fantastic vehicle for releasing the weight of the past but if you are in counselling year after year talking about the same issues, you are not healing, you are addicted to your story. You have decided to adorn the cloak of the victim. There, despite your larger than life protestations, is where you are content to stay.

I realise that this might seem harsh. I can hear the rants of protests as I type, but I can honestly assure you that we all have choice. We can choose to look at the pain, and then let it go. Or we can choose to revisit the pain at every available opportunity and allow it to linger and weave its way into our lives.

I naively thought everyone wanted to heal. After many

years of working with clients I have come to understand that this is not always the case. I have seen clients come to that place of choice. They stand in the middle ground between the old version of themselves that is hurt, wounded and familiar, and the new version of themselves that is boundless potential waiting to be released. What do they do? Sometimes they chose the old version. It is comfortable, and they know it intimately. They are afraid to give up their old identity. They are fearful that, if they choose the new version, they might fail. So better to stay with what you have than to make a fool of yourself by trying something new. The irony is that you cannot fail at being the new you because it is your essence waiting to be experienced and realised in the world.

Another aspect of choosing the new you is that your world will change. People that were friends with the 'wounded you' will often not want to be friends with the 'new you', because in effect you are a different person. You reflect to them the ability to change, but they have convinced themselves that they are quite content to stay exactly where they are. Hanging out with the new you makes them uncomfortable, because it causes cracks in the illusion that they have constructed for themselves.

So why choose the new you?

In reality you don't. It chooses you. From deep within you it rises up. It can be a feeling that 'all is not well'.

It can be an emotion: "I'm unhappy". It can be a sense "something is not right here". Or it can be more subtle. Often it is intangible. It is like the tectonic plates of your soul are shifting. You know something is moving but you don't know what. You feel unsettled, perhaps emotional, for no apparent reason, but something is stirring within. This is the new you; the aspect of you that remembers. It is your Divine Spirit, and it is calling you. It is calling you forward to the reality where the healed (and whole) version of you already exists. Sometimes we ignore the call. We party harder, drink more, and shout louder about how hurt, abandoned or tired we are. But it is patient. It can wait. It has been waiting for you since before you were born. And so it persists.

It calls out to you in dreamtime, bringing books to your attention. It allows you to overhear, per chance, a casual conversation that triggers a memory or an emotion. And still it waits until the longing inside you is so strong it eventually brings you to the water of life and asks you to drink. But are you willing? The new you expects much from you. It expects you to be your Greatness. It expects you not to be 'woe is little me', but 'Divine Me' expressing yourself to the world in all your magnificence.

Are you ready? Are you ready for new growth? Are you ready to extend yourself beyond the familiar; beyond the comfortable, so that you can see the new horizons, the new experiences and the new loving people that are available to you?

Some of you will say 'Yes' and rush to the river to drink. Some of you will say 'No'. Neither is right and neither is wrong. You must do what is right for you. But if you say 'no', we must alas part company, for this is a journey to wholeness, and to get there you must be willing to leave the 'old you' behind.

The more opportunities we give ourselves to remember the easier it is to choose the new you. In remembering we call forth our essential essence, and the stronger the essence the greater the momentum for moving forward. In time the new you becomes such an integral part of you that it is not the new you anymore. It is simply you.

Each time we remember, we send new roots down into the fertile soil of our becoming. We pull forth an energetic pulse that will stimulate new growth.

Remembering (which is the process of remembering your dismembered self) is an important part of the healing process. Remembering is answering our soul's calling to be one in the essence; in the image and likeness of the Divine.

You may wonder why you need to be one with the Divine. You may not be interested in following a spiritual path and that is fine. But if you are reading this book something has called you; something that runs deeper than you can imagine; something that has yet to unfold.

We have called it the garden, your inner glorious juicy self. You can call it Spirit, Krishna or Nirvana. You can call it inner peace or freedom. The name is irrelevant. It is merely a label onto which we can hang the metaphor of our becoming. What is relevant is that you are a seeker; a seeker who is looking to become whole. So let's remember together. In doing so let us call forward the Divine energy with which you entered this world. It is an energy that has, in many cases, been forgotten, yet an energy that is ready for her story to unfold.

Exercise – Visiting the Red Tent

- For the following exercise you will need your notebook and a pen.
- Take some deep breaths and allow your body to relax.
- Engage all your senses; your sight, your sense of smell, taste, touch and hearing. Consciously engage your intuition.
- In your minds eye imagine yourself sitting in the Red Tent.
- Look around. What is it like? What other women are there?
- How old are you? How do you feel? What can you hear? What does it smell like?
- What language do these women speak? What country are you in? What clothes are you wearing?

- Take your time to look around and experience your surroundings. If you cannot see anything, ask yourself: what do you intuitively know about this place?
- When you get a sense of this place open your eyes, take up your notebook and pen, and write your story of the Red Tent beginning with:
- "Once upon a time, in a faraway land, I sat in a circle of women in a Red Tent …"
- Let the story write itself. Do not force it. Let the words come. It doesn't have to make sense. If you have resistance, simply notice it. Remember to keep breathing, and let it pass. There is a story inside you waiting to be told.

Springtime

After my tumultuous transition from media executive to psychic, my partner, made all my romantic fantasies come true. He brought me to Paris for my birthday, and while standing at the top of the Eiffel Tower he asked me to marry him. Shortly afterwards, surrounded by our closest friends, we literally had a fairytale wedding.

We had our wedding in an old castle on a misty spring day. I was dressed like a gothic princess, in ivory and gold, with a deep crimson velvet cloak. He met me at the altar, looking in everyway like my prince charming. We had been together eleven years on the day we got married. As we banqueted with our family and friends we committed to spending the rest of our lives together. Like all good fairy stories all was not quite as it seemed.

It was a regular occurrence for the conversation at work to turn to sex. At first I used to find this both interesting and refreshing. Interesting that women talked about such things and refreshing that it made the whole topic open and accessible. It wasn't dirty, it wasn't taboo. It was life experience being shared. But I wasn't sharing. The more they talked, the worse I felt. I was listening to women talk about their partners, their lovers, and their orgasms. I felt like a pawn in some sick universal joke; an outsider that had no place being there.

I had never experienced a problem making love. I would get aroused, enjoying the waves of passion as they coursed through me building to a crescendo. Just before the peak (that ultimate toe tingling, nail curling orgasm that every woman's magazine ensures you that you can have), I would ... bottom out. It was like the energy would die. I was there, almost at the finish line. And then a big fat nothing.

I had long since resigned myself to the fact that this was the way things were; that it was normal; that it was probably the same for most women. As I didn't talk to any women about it I had no personal evidence to the contrary. That was until I went to work at The Haven. The more I listened, the more anguish I felt. Part of me desperately wanted to experience what they were experiencing. Part of me was hugely frustrated that I couldn't. The old me who couldn't orgasm was pitched in battle with the new me who really wanted to. One day I cracked. You guessed it; more tears, more wailing, but new resolve.

I went back to counselling. I wasn't sure if I consciously chose my new counsellor, or that she consciously chose me. It was one of those supposed 'chance' meetings in life, which you come to realise was set up by the Universe.

My counsellor explained to me that the ability to have an orgasm was in the 'Do Not Disturb' file where I had put my experience of being molested. To heal one, I had to be willing to go back and revisit the other.

I had done quite a bit of work around the issue of being molested. But what I had also done was put a very clever defence mechanism in place. This defence mechanism was called 'I will always be in control'. I rarely got drunk, because I didn't like the feeling of not being in control, and that someone else might be able to assert their control over me. Being in control was something I had incorporated into nearly every aspect of my life. In counselling I came to understand two important things. Firstly, if I wanted to have an orgasm I needed to let go of control, because one cannot coexist with the other. Secondly, I came to understand what happened as that orgasmic energy started to build.

As I recounted the process to my counsellor, I realised

that, before the point of release, where I could orgasm, I would energetically leave my body. If you have never experienced it, it is a bit like being outside of your body, looking back at yourself. What I also realised was that I had done this for the first time when that man came into my room and molested me. It had been my defence mechanism, so that I wouldn't get hurt, and I had been doing it ever since. The thing was that I didn't want to do it anymore. Having an orgasm is a very physical experience, and if you want to have one, you have to be in your body. And I really wanted to have one.

My counsellor was a wise and practical woman. I needed to retrain my body and my psyche. But I couldn't do it with my husband. I had too much of an expectation built into love making. I was caught in the cycle of desperately wanting to orgasm, and the huge frustration and disappointment that followed when I couldn't. She sent me off on a mission.

I have been to a lot of workshops and I have taken a lot of classes. But I can honestly tell you one of the greatest healings in my life came from a vibrator. The whole experience of acquiring my new found friend is a bit of a blur. It was a mixture of mortification, excitement, anticipation and "Please God don't let me meet anyone I know."

What followed was an amazing experience. Initially, I felt incredibly uncomfortable and self conscious but as

I lay there on my own I was able to conduct an experiment in the energy of orgasm. I was able to track the energy as it built in my body. I came to recognise the place where the intensity of the energy would build, and where I would have to make a choice; choose to shut down the energy, choose to leave my body, or choose to go with it and let go of control. In the beginning, I chose the old way. The energy was too intense, and I was afraid. I don't know what I was afraid of; afraid of letting go of something that I was so used to, or afraid of what the new 'me' might be like. I think there was a part of me that was afraid, that if I did let go, I might not be able to orgasm. And then what?

After many trial runs, one day something shifted. I felt the energy build. I breathed. I breathed, I remained in my body. And just when I thought I couldn't take the intensity of the energy anymore, I broke through what felt like a plate glass wall. Waves and ripples of energy ran through my body. And then, as I basked in bliss, I remembered. I remembered, as a child all the times that I had felt like this. Innocent play had often released this beautiful electrifying energy within me. I remembered the man in my room, and knew that he no longer had control over me. I remembered feeling self conscious and shameful of my body as a young teenager. I remembered it all. And as I remembered the pain, and the hurt washed through me, I felt another part of me rush back to life. I felt like I had reclaimed my womanhood, and my birthright.

Springtime is the season of new growth. That which has been resting all winter raises its head above the earth and prepares, once more, to share itself with the world. The spring colours, the yellows, whites and soft greens, bring forth the promise of new life and new beginnings. We too must step into the spring energy of our journey. We must unleash that which has been hidden, repressed, stored away or long forgotten. It is a wonderful time. The air is filled with potential. The hardness of the frost is replaced with the delicateness of the snowdrop. The dark mornings are brightened by the soft glow of the primrose.

It is a magical time, as, after the death of winter, we witness the world proclaiming its rebirth. When it comes to our own rebirth, the mind, for all its prowess, is often a disadvantage. The mind colludes with the ego. It needs to be rational, and it colludes with our belief systems. Instead, we need to bypass the mind and like a child, enter into the realm of emotion. We need to be ready to experience, to feel and to be surprised.

You have started to compost your rot, and you have begun to remember the essence of who you are. Now, before we follow those stepping stones into the garden, we must awaken the seeds that are buried in your soil.

Exercise – Awakening your Inner Seeds.

For this exercise you will need three sensual or evocative pieces of music. Not music that you like to dance around the kitchen to. Not music that reminds you of a past lover or a first date. You want music that stirs your soul; music that, when it's played, causes a rippling of energy through your body. You want to use music that will unlock the doors to your emotions, and life force energy that may have been suppressed for a while.

In choosing the music, what you want to do is pick music that washes through you like a wave. As the music washes through, it will talk to your emotions; your core energy. It will break open the hard seed pod, so that whatever is contained within can be released. It might be tears or laughter. It might be sensuality or rage. It might be love or fear. Do not engage with the emotion. Just allow it to wash through. You then become a vessel for growth; a vessel that we can lovingly tend to in the garden.

- Make three appointments with yourself. Pick a time when you will not be disturbed. Choose one piece of music per appointment. You may wish to light a candle. Make sure the room is warm.
- Lie or sit down, but don't be so comfortable that you will fall asleep. Make sure the music is loud enough to

fill the room. Loud enough that you can lose yourself in the music, but not so loud that it hurts, or damages your ears.

- Take three deep breaths, drawing them down the length of your body.
- Close your eyes.
- Relax into the music, and allow it to wash through you.
- Try not to analyse the process.
- Notice the places in your body where you have resistance or irritation.
- Notice when an emotion comes up to be released, and then let it go.
- Remember we are trying to disengage the mind.
- Allow your emotional body to do the work.
- After each session, in your journal make some notes about your experience.
- Notice any differences within yourself over the coming days as your seed pod cracks, and observe what emerges.

A Bud Blossoms

I felt like I had finally gained entry to an exclusive club. If I was an army general, I would have proudly worn my stripes on my shoulder, showing off to the world the badge of honour that I had just attained. There was a club called womanhood, and now, at last, I felt like I was in it.

I had new found confidence. I was one of 'the girls' and it was great. So it came as a huge surprise that, one day, as I was driving in my car Joseph appeared beside me. Since I stopped resisting him he only appeared during work or in my meditation.

"It's time for me to go", he said, "Our time together is done."

I felt like someone had punched me in the gut. Not because I was worried about work or clients, but because as well as being my guide, he was also my friend. He had guided me through my growing pains, and witnessed my early mistakes. When I was floundering with my own insecurities he was my rock, and now he was going. And I knew he meant it.

Heartbroken, I made an appointment with my friend Sinead. She had supported me when I had started my journey with Joseph and I knew there was no one more suited to holding space for me as he departed. When I arrived, the treatment room where she worked was dark, and lit by the soft glow of amber candle light. It was warm and cosy like a womb. I don't remember what we said, or if we spoke. She knew how hard this was for me, and she was there to support me all the way.

I lay on her plinth and she helped me to relax. She guided me into the most beautiful meditation. We travelled back to a temple in Egypt, where Joseph and I had first agreed to work together, and in that beautiful sacred space we said goodbye. I cried. I cried like my soul was about to break. I cannot begin to explain the love I felt for him, or he for me. While I knew it was right to say goodbye, I was so sad that our time together had ended. I felt like we had journeyed together through lifetimes and once again we had been called to part. We embraced and then in a heartbeat he was gone. When my awareness drifted back into the room, I looked at Sinead. Her eyes were full of love and compassion. "He is beautiful", she said. And he was. He was a beautiful, wise, and gentle soul.

I was fragile, and nervous of returning to work. How would I read if I had no guide to depend on? What would I do if I went blank, or had nothing to say? A very wise friend of mine uses a wonderful analogy when she is encouraging people to change. She talks about juggling. Apparently, the hardest part to juggling is not catching the third ball. It's letting go of the second ball so that there is room for something new (in this case the third ball) to come into your life.

In letting go of Joseph, despite the pain, something new came into my life. Initially, it was a new female guide. I think that, in retrospect, she was there to stop me having a panic attack in those early sessions, after Joseph's departure. She and I never truly bonded. She did, however, teach me to read in a different way. She explained to me that, if I connected directly to source, that it was not necessary to have an intermediate. She guided me, in new ways, to set my intention and call in Divine helpers. She encouraged me, in my ability, to trust in my gift, and be a channel for Spirit.

Still, I grew restless. When I read for clients I could see what was happening in their energy system, and what was causing it. I could provide them with a healing map.

Yet part of me felt like I wanted to be able to do more. They had information, but so what? How could they use that information to help themselves heal?

I had for the longest time wanted to go to Machu Picchu in Peru. A colleague of mine had visited there. From the time I saw her holiday photos I knew I wanted to go. As autumn rolled around, my husband and I, like two migrating birds took flight for South America.

It's a well worn cliché, but once we left behind the frantic energy of Lima, part of me felt like I had come home. We headed for Cusco, high in the mountains. It is the gateway for all travellers who wish to explore Peru's many sacred and ancient sites.

As languages go I find Spanish difficult. I am much more comfortable with the softer and more lyrical tones of Italian and French. Yet high up, as we strolled through the streets of Cusco I found it easy to understand and make myself understood. Spanish is spoken in a less harsh way, and at a gentler pace, which in some ways, I feel, reflects the people of Peru.

We explored the Sacred Valley, and I became enchanted with the Peruvians relationship with Pacha Mama (Mother Earth). Before they drank they offered her some of what was in their glass. They treated her with reverence, respect and kindness. Their connection with her had survived the test of time, and the Conquistadors. Being Irish, I also think part of me felt an affinity with the Peruvians. We are both conquered peoples who have lost much of their language and traditions at the hands of another, and we both love potatoes!

Before visiting Machu Picchu we headed into to the jungle to spend some time in the rain forest. Our guide said we would be brought to the river port of Puerto Maldonado where we would take a boat to our camp. I had assumed we would arrive at a regular port, with sizeable ships which would then take us on the five hour boat ride up the Madre de Dios, a tributary of the Amazon.

Forgetting that we were in South America we arrived at what can only be described as a scene from 'The African Queen'. The port consisted of some wooden poles at the side of the river, to which the boats were tied. Our boat, while having a small engine, resembled more of a canoe with a tarpaulin than an ocean liner. This was our transport to the jungle. In truth it was gorgeous. As we put-putted through the water we saw plants and wildlife emerge from the jungle. It was like a scene from a wildlife documentary. It was alive and enchanting and we were slap bang in the middle of it.

As I have mentioned before, there are key moments in our life that shape who we are, and what we are to become. For me, the jungle was one of those moments. I will never forget it. At night there was a blanket of stars above us. Under the tree canopy it was so black that you could not even see your hand in front of your face. There was a cacophony of noise that surrounded me all day and all night, as nature sang her song. I loved it. I loved absolutely everything about it, including the pungent smells and the sticky heat.

Our guide took us for a walk to show us the jungle's healing plants. It was nature's pharmacy on your doorstep. I was overcome by the wisdom of Pacha Mama, and Great Spirit. Everything you needed was here. All you needed to know was how to find it; fruit, nuts, herbs, meat and shelter. Mother Earth provided it all for you. All she asked was that you take no more than you needed, and give something back in return.

One day, as we were walking through the jungle, something unusual happened. In the blink of an eye I was no longer with my group. Instead, the people that walked in front of me, although from the jungle, were of a different time. They looked like hunters and tribal people. I cried. I don't know why I cried. I think that, perhaps, my soul reconnected with a part of itself. It was a part that had long been forgotten, and was so glad to be home. Yet, in that instant, I knew why I had come to Peru. There was a part of me that needed to remember. I knew what I had to do. And then, as quickly as it happened, it was gone. I was back among my fellow travellers, walking single file through the jungle.

Many traditions talk about the veil between the worlds. It is the space between past and present where, spirit world and 'real' world is so thin that you can walk right through. One of the most famous times for the veil being thin is 'All Hallows Eve', or Halloween. The reason it is said that we dress up in disguise is because the spirits from the other side of the veil can cross over to our world to capture souls. We dress up to confuse the spirits, so that we look like one of their own. In doing so, we evade capture. That day, in the jungle, I think I stepped between the veils. I stepped into a time past where I had once belonged. That may be truth, or fanciful conjecture on my part. Either way it marked the beginning of a new and beautiful chapter in my life.

On returning home I knew I wanted to study Peruvian Shamanism. It was like I had found the missing piece in a puzzle. It connected my love of Spirit with my love of nature. It combined my ability to 'see' with my desire to help people heal. This was the next step on my path.

Shamanism is one of the oldest forms of healing in existence, dating back to prehistoric times, with roots across the globe, including the Americas, Siberia, Australia, Indonesia, parts of Europe and Africa. The shaman would have been the medicine man or woman in the tribe. They could commune with the spirit world. They used the information they received for many things including healing. Studying Peruvian Shamanism was, however, easier said than done. For a start, I didn't know any shamans. I knew people who had studied shamanism, but all their teachers had trained in the North American tradition. I needed to find a teacher. And so I prayed.

A friend of mine gave me a book called *Shaman, Healer, Sage* by Alberto Villoldo. Villoldo is a classically trained medical anthropologist who has studied shamanic healing techniques among the Q'ero, the descendants of the ancient Incas, for over 25 years. As I read his descriptions of what Alberto calls the luminous body, I realised that this was what I saw when I read for clients. Someone else saw what I saw. He had beautiful techniques to help me to work with the luminous body; to help clients heal and come back to wholeness. Then I heard that for the first time ever, Alberto was coming to Ireland to share this beautiful medicine. My teacher, two months after I had gotten back from Peru, had appeared.

Alberto was giving an introductory talk in a hotel, on the outskirts of Dublin. To get to the hotel from where I lived meant that I had to enter the evening commuter traffic. The journey normally took at least an hour and it was a dark and wet November night. Even though I had prayed for a teacher I felt huge resistance to going. I also knew that he was going to do a soul retrieval with the group that night. The part of me that had been through counselling and healing questioned as to whether I wanted to open myself up for more of the same again.

I decided not to go. The universe, however, had already outsmarted me. The phone rang and it was my friend, Sinead. We had agreed to go to the talk along with another friend of ours. Before I had a chance to take a breath she announced down the phone "It's a really bad night. There is no point us all going separately, so I will collect you and we can all travel together". And like a flash of lightening she was gone.

My stomach was knotted all the way in the car. On a night where the traffic should have been slower than a death march we miraculously arrived at the hotel in about forty minutes. We were so early that, when we got to the seminar room, there was hardly anyone there. In marched Sinead, with me dragging my heels behind, and up she walked to the top of the room where there were lots of empty seats. Looking very content with herself, she ushered us into the best seats in the house.

There we sat in the front row. Waiting for who knew what, and then he arrived, a gentle man, with deep soft eyes. From the moment he spoke I knew that this was my path, and that I would do the training. Towards the end of the night, as promised, Alberto guided the assembled group through a soul retrieval. I have been told the greater the resistance the bigger the gift. That night was one of life's gifts. Not only was the soul retrieval one of the sweetest gentlest healings that I had ever experienced, but Spirit had marked coordinates on my map and I knew the direction I needed to follow.

The training that followed was truly amazing. It was based on the principles of the Peruvian Medicine Wheel, an age old system of personal transformation. The medicine wheel is not exclusive to Peru. It is found in many cultures, and while the format may vary the teachings are often the same. The medicine wheel helps you to free yourself from your personal woundings (your story) so that you can align yourself to Spirit, and with your heart. In doing so, you become available for life. You leave behind the binding energy that inhibits us from having loving relationships with our fellow wo/man and the Earth.

I have participated in many groups, and inevitably there is a mix of personalities who clash. When I started the training there were some people that I did not particularly like, and a few who terrified me. By the end of our two years together there was not one person out of over sixty people who I did not enjoy sitting and chatting with. Not all would become close friends, but in dealing with my projections, and my woundings the energy of irritation that had prevailed towards some of my fellow students in the early days had disappeared. You learned to look beyond the woundings and see the soul that lived within.

I relished the shamanic path. Everything about it sang to my soul. I loved the healing techniques. I loved that it honed my ability to see. I loved the connection with nature and the Divine. I quickly introduced the techniques to my clients, and loved being able to offer them more than a healing map. It seems that all the experiences that had happened since my breakdown were allowing me to blossom into something, and someone new.

Back into the Earth

There is a wonderful old joke:

Q: 'How do you make God laugh?'
A: 'Tell him your plans'

I thought I had it all sewn up. I was married, living with my husband and my dogs close to the sea. I had a good healing practice and I was teaching workshops. All in all life seemed good. As far as I was concerned, I had arrived. I had experienced a difficult time, learned from it over the years and changed my direction in life. I now worked for myself (and God) and was quite content that life would progress this way until the end of my time. I realise now that this is actually rest time. It is during the rest time that you get to integrate all that has happened to you before God decides that you are ready for your next growth spurt. Hence the joke!

So there I was, sitting in a master's class with some of my shamanic peers, and someone started to talk about Goddesses. As the conversation progressed two of the participating women started to look around the room, and named the women they felt epitomised Goddess energy. I sat there feeling very self assured, waiting to hear my name as their gaze came to my side of the room. I heard them mention my friend, a fiery Polish Taurean. I heard them mention a woman who was several seats away. What I didn't hear was my name. It wasn't like they thought about me and dismissed me at the last moment for not quite making the cut. It became very clear that I wasn't even in the running.

I was gob smacked. It was like being the kid in the playground who nobody wanted in their team. I felt that there was a confidence and sexiness about me. I considered myself womanly. It seemed, however, that while I may have graduated into the orgasm club, the Goddess circle was somewhat more elusive. Nobody likes being an outsider, so in that instant, I decided to figure out how to gain entry.

What followed was an incredible journey into the

unknown, and a timely remembering. I had naively thought that being a woman automatically made you a Goddess. Now that this particular belief system had been well and truly shattered I needed to find out what a Goddess was, and how I could become one. Initially a process that I thought might involve buying a new lipstick and an eye liner turned out to be an exploration, and awakening, of the essence of womanhood that lives within us all.

I've searched hard to find the words within me that could convey to you the energy of the Goddess, if you have had no previous experience of it. I have struggled, wrestled and been overwhelmed with frustration. But no words can convey the energy I wish to describe. It is instead a transmission, like a loving gaze passed from one lover to another without words. It is the feeling a mother has when she sees the smile of her child. No words are necessary, as the emotion felt communicates all necessary information.

From my desk, however, I cannot look into your eyes and show you the fire of the Goddess that burns within me. You cannot see me kick off my shoes and watch the energy of the Goddess ooze from my very being as I dance. Instead I am endeavouring to provide you with words that will paint a landscape into which you can place yourself, and observe the energy of the Goddess for yourself. This is a journey of exploration.

The Goddess energy that you will eventually hold is different to the energy that I have come to embody.

The Goddess is like a garden, with many beautiful flowers, each with their unique scent. One flower is not more beautiful than another. All of them have their own characteristics. Some flowers blossom in spring and some in autumn. Some have smooth leaves and some have barbs on the stems. Each radiant flower holds the energy of all flowers; divine beauty made manifest. And yet one flower on its own cannot convey the beauty of the species as a whole. But on its own it is still perfect and complete. This is the energy of the Goddess, varied, even though there is a common theme, complex and at the same time beautifully simple.

How will you know when you have connected with the energy? How do you know when you are in love? It is a feeling that is indescribable and yet completely tangible. Other people will know that you have connected with it. They will notice that something has changed, but they will not be able to put their finger on it. "Have you changed your hair?", "What's different about you?" they will ask. But you will know. Your inner Goddess has been reawakened from her long and arduous sleep.

The principle of the Goddess is multifaceted. In our modern world we have often come to think of a goddess as merely a sexy woman, and while that is an element of the Goddess, the energy in its essence, is much more complex. No one really knows the true starting point of both the Goddess as God and the Goddess as an archetype. Research has uncovered much interesting material that dates back to prehistoric times. It has been said that the Goddess is the creator, and that Goddess archetypes are the various manifestations of this creatrix energy. This is in no way a concise anthology of Goddess history or myth. It is merely a starting point for you to explore further, a triggering stimulus for you to unleash the Goddess that is perhaps trapped, buried or hidden within. It is necessary, on your journey to your own inner Goddess, to discern what the energy means to you.

Back when the world was young, our brothers and sisters took great time, and cared to observe all that was around them. They observed the seasons, day break and sunset. They observed the crops, and how and where they grew. They observed when the rivers would swell and when the temperature of the ocean would change. They were watchers, and over time they became experts in observing nature. They watched each other too, and how as a tribe they grew old or sick and died; how new life came into the world replacing tribe members that had been lost. In the process of watching they saw that everything occurred in cycles; cycles of life and death. After the death of what we now call winter came the new life of springtime. After the death of an elder or a tribe member, there was always new life, new birth. And so the cycle of life continued.

As they watched they became aware that the cycle of life was a feminine principle. It was the women of the tribe who gave birth to their sons and daughters. It was the female of the animals, that they tracked and hunted, that gave birth to offspring. In noticing the cycles of life and death they came to know the earth as feminine, as she too gave life. She offered up the new seasons. She birthed the crops. The rivers, lakes and oceans sprang from her belly. The hot lava, when it erupted burst forth from between the legs of the earth, like a woman in labour. The earth became their mother, giving life to all, and as such she was respected, honoured and worshiped.

This feminine principle was also noticed in its rawest form in nature. A mother lion would fight to the death to protect her cubs. She nurtured her young and then encouraged their independence. Female animals and birds engaged in courtship, and watched the displays of masculine prowess while being wooed to mate. The feminine was observed to be caring and compassionate; wise and intuitive; and passionate, fierce and loving. Over time this feminine principle came to be called Goddess, the feminine counterpart to the male God energy of creation.

Each energy was equal; Mother & Father God, God & Goddess, Ying & Yang, Divine Masculine & Sacred

Feminine. The world was observed in relation to these principles. In some traditions, soft rolling mountain ranges that resembled the curves of a woman's body were deemed feminine. High mountain peaks that resembled phalluses were considered masculine. Offerings were made to 'God & Goddess' to keep these energies in balance and in harmony, for when the divine principles were in harmony so too was the earth.

The Goddess has many names. Some of them include the Creatrix, Mother Earth and Pacha Mama. The name is irrelevant. The Goddess in her many forms is the Divine Feminine energy of creation. She is receptive, passionate, creative, energetic, intuitive, fertile, strong, nurturing, abundant, patient, wise, sensual and sexual.

The characteristics of the Goddess are so varied. In an attempt to honour and invoke different aspects of this energy we see the emergence of the Goddess archetype, and Goddess worship. The ancients worshipped the Goddess in her many forms. They made offerings to the rivers, the mountains and the land. This worship was not always healthy. Man, at times, forgot that the mother is always loving, even to her most errant of children. So at times when they had forgotten her love they sacrificed their own kind, or the yet unborn, to appease her, and beg for her approval. But a mother does not need to be appeased. A lioness may scold her young but she always welcomes them back to the pride.

The Goddess archetype was divided into Goddesses, each one embodying different aspects of the Universal Goddess. There were Goddesses who looked after the crops, courtship, fertility, childbirth and abundance, etc. Whatever energy or protection you wished to invite into your life, you prayed to the relevant Goddess. Each culture had their own Goddesses which incorporated the myths and legends of their people.

One of the most famous Goddesses is probably Aphrodite, the Greek Goddess of love and beauty.

Spider Grandmother is a Native American Goddess who her people consider to be the creator of the world. She has power to give and take life, and is associated with hunting and agriculture. She is also said to have taught the Native Americans how to weave. Some stories say that she is also responsible for the stars. She spun a web and laced it with morning dew. She then threw the web up into the sky, and the sparkle of the dew became the stars.

The Celtic Goddess Brigid is the Goddess of fire, in the forge and in the hearth. She is also the Goddess of poetry, healing and childbirth. When Brigid's eternal flame burns within, you are able to unleash your creativity, passion and healing ability. She is also the Goddess who looks after many of the sacred wells in the Celtic World. The water from these wells is considered to have healing properties.

Another aspect of the Goddess archetype is the triple Goddess; Maid, Mother and Crone. The Maid represents the youthful aspect of the Goddess. She is carefree, wild, passionate and adventurous. The Mother is nurturing, gentle, protective and watchful. The Crone is wise, restful, bluntly honest and often wickedly humorous. The adventurous nature of the Maid makes her worldly. It allows her to explore her personality and search for a mate. The somewhat selfish nature of the Maid finds maturity as she enters the stage of motherhood, where she learns compassion and unconditional love. When the woman enters her Crone phase, her menstrual blood ceases and she becomes an elder in the tribe; sharing the wisdom of her experience as Maid and Mother, with all the women who surround her. As she no longer bleeds she has time to teach, and pass on the skills and stories of her tribe. The phase of the Crone is also an important time for reflection; to reflect on ones life before making the transition into the next phase, death.

The triple Goddess represents the cycle of womanhood, but there is also much more significance to this archetype. The symbolic representation of the Goddess, the triple spiral, also represents the menstrual cycle of women.

The menstrual cycle is a monthly representation of the cycle of birth and death. An egg is released, prepared for fertilisation, and when pregnancy doesn't occur, the egg dies, and the lining off the womb falls away. The womb is cleansed and prepared for the cycle to begin again. In communities where women live together their natural cycle will often fall into rhythm with each other, and they will menstruate together.

The energy of the Maid is compared to the menstrual cycle, post menses through to ovulation. You have more vitality and enthusiasm. This is often a good time to start a project, as you have that 'get up and go' energy.

The energy of the Mother is apparent at the time of ovulation. You are receptive and creative, open to a partner and mate. Women often notice that their desire for sex increases at this time. If you are not actively trying to get pregnant, this is a good time to pour your creative energies into a project, and actively 'mother' what is important in your life.

The energy of menstruation is the energy of the Crone. The Crone embodies death, and letting go. This is the time to withdraw, go within and let go of what no longer serves you. This is an opportune time to finish projects. Your intuition is at its peak, and you will often have vivid dreams.

Biologically, as we age, we naturally pass through the various stages of the triple Goddess. But isn't it amazing that we can also access different aspects of the triple Goddess at the various stages of our menstrual cycle? Even if you are post menopausal, and in the 'croneship' of your life, you still have access to the other elements of the Goddess. Once embodied, the triple Goddess lives within, and is no longer an outward projection, or a distant concept. In honouring our bodies, we honour the cycles of life, ourselves as women and the earth.

As powerful as the energy of the triple Goddess is, most of us have been cut off from it. The separation of women from the wisdom of the Goddess has led to generations of women who have lost their sense of self and their sense of connection to the Divine Feminine.

There has been much discussion as to why this happened. Some say that women started to abuse their power and tried to dominate men. Men became fearful, and in retaliation began to circulate rumours that women were sorceresses and should not be trusted. This caused what were once considered the gifts of the feminine, her intuition and strength to be reviled and feared. Some point a finger to the evolution of the Christian church. As its teachings progressed it condemned sensuality and sexuality two of the traits of the feminine to be sinful and shameful. Some say that, as the world is cyclical in nature, it is natural that over time we changed from a matriarchal society, when the feminine was honoured, to a patriarchal society. Once more the world turns, but this time we witness the birth of a new paradigm, where the masculine and feminine will coexist in harmony.

There is no simple explanation as to why the beauty of

the Divine Feminine is no longer revered and honoured. Anthropologists, sociologists, psychotherapists and theologians, among others, have written tomes as to why they believe the Divine Feminine was no longer seen as sacred. You could spend lifetimes reading all the available material on the subject. While I believe that this information is incredibly valuable as a study, I think there is little value in lingering in the past. Our planet is at crisis point. Daily, we pollute the Divine Feminine; we rape her forests and poke holes in her sky. We no longer hold each other in the energy of nurturing love. Instead, we live in a world of fear and suspicion. If our world is to change we need to change our relationship to the feminine within. We need to honour her in all her radiant glory, and in doing so bring change and healing to our world, and to ourselves.

As women have attempted to compete with men instead of living in harmony with them, we have removed ourselves from the natural cycle of life. Our 'Sacred Blood' is called 'the curse', an unwanted visitor in our hectic lives. Advertising blitzes us with the latest painkillers and products that will ensure our lives won't have to be inconvenienced by this messiness. We talk of it as an affliction. Instead of stopping, withdrawing and honouring this mystical time, we force ourselves to keep going and appear 'normal'. What is normal is to honour this magical experience, and use this time to connect to wisdom that dwells deep within you.

Many women think severe pain, cramps and clotting are all part of menstruation. They are not. These are symptoms that tell you that you are out of sync with your natural cycle. Some mild discomfort is natural. Your blood should be a rich, fluid, ruby red. You may feel the desire to be on your own, or to be reflective at this time. If you wish to connect with your inner Goddess, connect with, and honour, the beauty of your menstrual cycle. It is a cycle that connects you to the heavens, and to the earth, and presents you with a unique gift as a species.

Any aspect of our psyche that is not honoured becomes toxic, and will, over time poison us. In shamanism and psychotherapy this is called the 'shadow'. Our shadow is that which we keep hidden, and are often too ashamed to look at for fear of admitting that it is part of our character. The more we hide and suppress it, the bigger it grows, until eventually it will mutate, and burst forth, calling for attention and wreaking havoc in our lives.

If the Maid aspect of your character has not been lived, she will often appear in your thirties. She will present herself as wild, reckless and bored. If you are married, or in a relationship, she may draw you into an affair, looking for that wild abandon that she never experienced in her youth. The shadow aspect of the

Mother is often smothering instead of nurturing. She doesn't allow her children to leave the nest, as she is fearful of the world and of being on her own.

The shadow of the Crone is resistance to aging and owning your wisdom. The desire to be eternally young becomes paramount. This is so evident in society today. We defy age at all costs. Anti wrinkle creams, botox and implants are commonplace as we rage war against the cycle of life. Instead of embracing our elders and their wisdom, we send them to nursing homes and retirement villages as outcasts from the community, so that we don't have to be reminded that aging and death is a natural cycle of life.

In recent years there has been much talk in society about the oppression of woman. The finger of blame has often been pointed first at man, and then at the institutions of religion. The most significant cause for the oppression of women is, in my opinion, women. The shadow aspect of the feminine is not pleasant. It is bitchy and judgmental. It is ruthless, and lacks compassion. The shadow aspect of the feminine literally eats her young.

When our own feminine is unlived we turn on each other. How often have you sat with your girlfriends or watched TV and talked about other women; "She is too fat, too thin", "Why is she wearing that?", "She is completely insincere", and "Who does she think she is?"

How often have you voiced similar utterances? It is like we are in some grand competition where only one of us can survive to attain the mate, the finances or the education. So instead of entering into hand to hand combat, as that is a masculine trait, we do something far more insidious. We start to belittle our feminine sisters. We tear apart their unique divine energy because it is different to our own. If we can get rid of the competition there will be more left of whatever you are looking or striving for.

This is a shadow aspect of the feminine and it is not pretty. It is also not how the universe works. In a rainforest each animal and plant is equally important. If you remove one species it affects the whole ecosystem of the forest. So too is it with life. We are unique, with beautiful individual talents and gifts. Some of us are great mothers, great teachers, great dancers, or great painters. When we sit together, and combine all our talents, we create a deep life-effusing well from which we can all drink and ultimately prosper and grow. When we cut ourselves and others off from this supply we become parched and die. Each nasty thing we say about other women is like dripping poison into the well of life.

The irony is that this verbal or mental assault on the Divine Feminine is actually an outward projection of a shadow that lives within you. It is a shadow aspect of your psyche that you don't wish to look at or own, but is begging for attention. The very nature of our shadow means that we cannot see it within ourselves. We have to project it onto something so that we can see it.

Start to take responsibility for all your thoughts. If you have negative thoughts don't push them down, as this only adds energy to them. Instead, bring them up into your consciousness, and when you hear yourself saying or thinking "She is ...", stop and ask yourself, "Why would I think that about myself?" Then you can start to tease out the answer.

I used to be livid about people that dumped their litter on the street. In taking ownership of the projection I was adamant that I always put my litter in rubbish bins. On teasing it out further I thought about my emotional litter. I had to admit to myself that I dumped my emotional trash on my family all the time. The beauty of watching your projections is that once you bring them up into the consciousness you will be provided with opportunities to heal them, and integrate that shadow aspect that has not until now had a voice.

The following exercises are designed to reconnect you with the Earth, the Divine Feminine and with your natural menstrual cycle.

Exercise – Bringing Light to the Shadows

- In your journal fill at least one full page with what you consider to be the positive attributes of women.
- Start each sentence with "Women are ..."
- Then fill at least one more full page with what you consider to be the negative attributes of women, starting each sentence with "Women are ..."

An inner shadow is both positive and negative. By doing the above exercise you are looking at the positive and negative aspects, as you perceive them, of the Divine Feminine. Ultimately you are looking at what you deem to be the positive and negative aspects of yourself. Do not judge yourself for what you have written but instead honour the fact that you are letting all aspects of yourself come up to the surface. In time you can choose which aspects you wish to embrace, and which ones you are ready to let go of, but for now bring all traits of the inner feminine to the surface.

Exercise – Back Into the Earth

- Go outside and kneel, or lie, on the earth.
- Take a few deep breaths, and centre yourself.
- Engage all your senses, and let your imagination and intuition run wild.

- Placing your hands on the Earth, on the belly of the Divine Mother, what does she feel like?
- Bringing your face right down onto the earth breathe in deeply.
- What does Pacha Mama, the Divine Feminine, smell like?
- Stick out our tongue; what does the Creatrix taste like?
- If you could visualise her as a woman in your minds eye, what would she look like?
- Turn your head sideways and listen; what does she say to you?
- Thank her for sharing herself.
- You may wish to make some notes in your journal about your experience.

Stepping Stones

After a period of working with my new guide, my other worldly helpers took on a different form. Instead of working with just one guide, a team of helpers would show up to help me with readings and healings. This team, I affectionately, and some would say irreverently, came to know as 'the Lads'. The Lads, in their essence, are a loving vibration, attuned to the frequency of the Christ Consciousness. They are old souls who have chosen, and have been chosen, to be guiding emissaries in our changing world. They were incarnate once, but a very long time ago, and their journey of service this time is to help mankind evolve.

They assist me when I work with clients but they also guide me in my personal life during meditation or when I call on them for help and guidance. While I can always see several of them at the same time and feel their presence, like a group of friends hanging out together, there is only ever one clear voice. It is neither masculine nor feminine, and yet not asexual, somehow holding the qualities of both sexes.

Their collective consciousness, although made up of different energies, always speaks to me as one, and yet it feels like more than one. One of my favourite traits of the Lads is their wicked sense of humour. Many a time they have brought a smile to my face with their quick wit.

The stepping stones that you are about to read were given to me by the Lads. I can honestly tell you that the Lads have never led me astray. They have shared information with me that I thought was 'off the wall'. But on presenting it to my clients, it has been pin point accurate.

The concepts that they present here are in some cases different to older and well respected teachings. In some cases the teachings are an amalgamation of previously established work. In all instances I believe that they are from the heart of consciousness and are preparing us for an unprecedented paradigm shift in our way of being.

Enjoy them as they take you on a beautiful journey into the realms of your own Inner Garden.

The First Stepping Stone
~ Awareness ~

"*Awareness that all is not well in your world, and that something needs to change.*"

Awareness is an interesting thing. Most of us have it, and very few of us use it. Many gurus tell us that once we live in a state of awareness much of the hardship of life disappears, as we begin to use that old cliché, and see the wood from the trees.

Many people think of awareness as a state of the mind. But this is not the case. Yes, there is a mental knowing, but this is often only the last stage of a more complex process. Think about a time when you were uncomfortable. It might have been when you were at a party, walking down the street, getting a train late at night, etc. Was it a mental state or a thought that lead to your discomfort? I am guessing it wasn't. I am guessing it was more of a body sense; a body knowing, that transcended the mind, and was more like a cellular feeling.

Awareness, in this context, is an energetic knowing that comes from deep within your being. It is heightened intuition. You can't describe it, or explain it, but there is no mistaking when you have it. If we bring our awareness, that deep body knowing, to any situation, we see the story behind the story. You don't see a grumpy waitress serving you morning coffee. Instead, you get a body sense that something is wrong with them. Perhaps you could offer a smile or a kind word, knowing that if the situation was reversed you would like someone to do the same for you.

Many years ago when I was out of college I worked as a sales assistant in a photography shop. One Wednesday afternoon I was there on my own and a guy came into the store. I got a body sense the minute I saw him. Then my mind observed that he was poorly dressed, and shifty. I had been studying positive thinking at the time, and in a nanosecond reprimanded myself for judging him on how he looked. I decided to be positive, and treat him politely like every other customer. He asked some questions about the cost of getting film processed, and left shortly afterwards. Thirty minutes later he returned, jumped over the counter and robbed me with a syringe.

Apart from the trauma of it all, this was one of the greatest lessons I've ever had. The second he walked in the door I had the awareness that something wasn't right. I didn't know (i.e. have the logic) that something was wrong, but I had a body sense. You may call this intuition, and yes, intuition is part of awareness, because intuition is the first gateway past the ego mind. But awareness is a deeper sense. Awareness, on some level, resonates with all your chakras, so that there is a whole body 'knowing/sensing' as opposed to intuition, which is a localised awareness in your third eye chakra.

It is important to understand awareness. In this context it is a deep soul and body knowing which is greater than the sum of the parts. If you talk to any woman whose husband or partner has had an affair, I guarantee you she will have had an awareness that something was going on. Now she may not have allowed her mind to actually join the dots together but somewhere deep inside her, she knew. Awareness it a bit like liquid mercury. It is there but if you try to touch it, it separates or rolls away, you just have to observe it for what it is.

When it comes to our own growth the initial stepping stone is awareness. This may seem incredibly simple but in fact we tend to suppress our awareness at every given opportunity. Awareness is a positive. It is our inner guidance system making us aware that we need to adjust our course. So why do we not embrace it with open arms. Often in adjusting our course, we have first to face a reality we would rather avoid and then make changes accordingly. Most of us are creatures of habit, we do not embrace or often desire change.

If your awareness is stirring you may need to change jobs, boyfriends, husbands or partners. You may need to be on your own for a while, to retreat from life, or you may need to step out into life. Awareness brings many challenges that we would sooner suppress to our hidden depths and ignore. We over eat, over medicate and over indulge so that we anaesthetise ourselves to our inner voice. Awareness is our inner compass that allows us to steer a course to our 'true' self, if we are willing to listening to it.

Awareness is the first stepping stone on your journey towards your inner garden because it is necessary to track within yourself where you feel out of kilter with your essential self and with the world. Awareness is subtle, it might reveal itself in sleepless nights, weight gain, funny feelings in your tummy that are nothing to do with indigestion, or a niggling thought or feeling that just won't go away.

Unless you have a relationship with yourself you will never know how and when your awareness is trying to make contact. The first thing you need to do is start to listen to your body. Know its physical essence. How does it respond if you push it too hard or exercise too much? How does it respond if you don't exercise? What foods does it like/dislike? Where is it happy and where is it safe? What does it like to do and what makes it uncomfortable? Be discerning; notice the nuances in everything you do and how your body responds accordingly.

Apply the same principle to your emotional body. What makes you feel happy and what makes you feel sad? What excites you? When do you feel numb? Does it take a lot to make you laugh or are you prone to outbursts of laughter. What makes you cry? What makes you moan? When do you get angry? Come to know your emotions and accept them for what they are. They are markers, bringing your attention to the rise and fall of energy in your body. Crying or laughing does not have a positive or negative charge. It is how we interpret the emotion, the filter through which we view it, that adds the charge. So spend time observing your emotions and see what caused them, how you feel about them and when is the last time you experienced the same thing.

Only when you know yourself will you be able to discern what awareness is and what is a regular body sense or emotion. Awareness at a soul level runs deep. It is like a stirring from deep within your core. Do not expect to understand it at first but in time it will reveal itself. If you open the channel to your deepest most inner wisdom, it is only a matter of time before it starts to flow through.

Don't be afraid to engage with your awareness, talk to it, like you would to a friend. Ask it to reveal itself, why has it come, and what does it want of you. The more you engage with it, the more it will develop and the less allusive it will appear. Do not be fearful that everything it needs to bring to your attention is bad. It will also draw your attention to what makes you feel good, alive and full of vitality. This is a deeper sense than just feeling at ease with the world. It is like every single cell in your body is beating to the pulse of your internal drum.

Imagine tribes women dancing around fires to drum music, this is the solid resonance that your awareness can connect you to when you are 'on track'. Similarly if all is not well in the garden, or if rot has set in, your awareness will stir and you will start to feel uncomfortable in your skin. A body sense will eventually shake to the surface irregularities in your life that are stopping you from being the true you. Some of these may be old beliefs, old programming, or old wounds. More often than not however it is a sense that something just doesn't quite fit, and a bit like a snake squirming to shed her old skin, you will be called to allow your essence to shine and release that which is no longer of value in your life.

Awareness is the calling card of the soul. It whispers

to you in the night. 'Come forth my sweet beauty and allow your light to shine. Do not hide under fear and self loathing, step forward into the night and experience the world anew'.

Exercise – Meeting your Body

- Over the coming weeks start to notice your body.
- How it looks and how it feels. Notice your thoughts.
- Are they predominately positive or negative?
- Who or what do you spend most of your time thinking about?
- Start noticing your emotions.
- What triggers them?
- Notice if there is a lot of sugar, alcohol or junk food in your diet, these all squash down your ability to connect with your awareness.
- Build a relationship with your emotional, physical and mental body.
- Embrace this new friendship like the return of a long lost friend.

Exercise – Meeting your Awareness

Awareness is not a by product of logic. So suspend your logic for approximately the next ten minutes. Let your imagination guide this exercise. Just go along with what ever images or words you get. There is no wrong and no right way to do this exercise. You will need to have your journal and a pen by your side to take notes afterwards.

- Sit comfortably, with your feet flat on the floor.
- Close your eyes and take some deep slow deliberate breaths.
- Allow your breath to sink right down into the core of your being.
- Keeping your eyes closed ask your inner body sense to show you an image that represents your awareness.
- It doesn't matter what the image is, it might be a shape, a colour, an animal etc. Whatever shows up is perfect.
- Go with the first thing that pops into your consciousness even if it seems off the wall.
- If you can't see it, just try and get a sense of what it would be if you could see it. Or perhaps instead of an image it might be a body sense, a sound or a smell.
- Thank your awareness for showing up, remember it's your long lost friend.
- Take a moment to get a sense of it.
- How does it look, feel, smell and sound? Is it healthy or is it in need of some attention?
- Is it friendly or feeling ignored?

- Ask your awareness has it anything to tell you at this time.
- And finally ask your awareness, what does it need from you.
- When you are done, thank your awareness and if you wish to do so you can arrange to meet it again.
- Take a few deep centring breaths before opening your eyes.
- Make some notes in your journal about your experience.
- Noticing if you had any resistance or if the experience was easy etc.
- Write down how you feel now, after doing the exercise.

The Second Stepping Stone
~ Self Appreciation ~

"*You must appreciate the Divine 'self'. God created the universe and you are part of the universe, therefore God also created you. This may seem simplistic but one of the main reasons we carry so many woundings and issues is that we believe we are separate from God. If we have been hurt, abandoned, abused etc. we often believe that God in that instance left us, and that we are not deserving of his abundant love. Anywhere in your life that you have an issue, be it a health issue, an emotional issue, a relationship issue or a financial issue, means that on some level you feel separate from God. Appreciating the Divine 'self' will not automatically heal the separation that exists in your psyche but it will start the internal process of questioning your beliefs which will help you step towards Oneness. In Oneness separation cannot exist. If separation cannot exist it is impossible to be at war with yourself because you are one with the Divine. The Divine is infinite love, masquerading as you."*

Self love and self appreciation are not new concepts. We know to encourage our young, tell them they are loved and provide with the enthusiasm and belief that everything is possible and attainable. When a young child is learning to walk we endlessly encourage them to keep putting one foot in front of the next, and when they stumble we quickly urge them to get right back up and try again. Over time their confidence grows. They gain balance and in what seems like moments. They leap from those tentative first steps to being able to run around the kitchen, relishing their new found freedom. Never once do we tell them that they can't do it. We don't ever say, "It's okay honey. Mommy will keep pushing you around in your stroller until you grow up." It's the experience of learning to walk that grows the child. The toddler will persevere until they perfect this new art, and the parent will encourage them every literal step of the way.

How do we transition from this place of wonderment to a place of futility within ourselves where we believe that we can't do it; where we are not good enough; where good things happen to other people but not to us? ... and on and on the list goes. Not only do we acquire these less encouraging new beliefs but we also forfeit giving ourselves the same encouragement that we would give to a child. So instead of simply saying "that just didn't work out, but I tried my best" we run the inner dialogue which says "I'm useless; I'm not doing that again". We wouldn't say this to a child but we frequently say this to ourselves.

The reasons we do not appreciate ourselves are many. In the earlier part of this book you already explored some of the experiences and the people that made a dent in your belief that you were a perfect child of God. In acquiring the belief that you were no longer a perfect child of God, you also probably took on the belief, albeit deep in your subconscious, that you were separate from God. If God is perfection and you are no longer perfection then you cannot be God. If you believe that you cannot be God, it is probably not too far a leap of faith to suggest that you are probably having a difficult time accepting that you are also a Goddess.

Part of the beauty of being human is that we are able to make mistakes. I am not keen on the word 'mistake'. I prefer to look on what we call mistakes as opportunities for growth. However I do accept that many of us walk through life feeling that we go from one mistake to another. Instead of considering these situations as mistakes think of them as divine opportunities to acquire new wisdom where we can grow and facilitate change. If we looked at them in that context we would probably feel very different about ourselves. Instead of saying "I'm a failure at relationships", observe what didn't work, and then see what you need to do so that you can go about doing it differently the next time.

As humans I believe that we are all doing the best we can based on the experiences we have had. I also believe that as humans we can change the inner filter through which we view every event that has occurred in our life, and in doing so change our feeling about the event and how we subsequently react to it. Regarding being molested I can choose to look at it several ways. I can choose to believe that the world is not a safe place, and believe that men only harm women, or I can choose to see sex as something hurtful, which causes emotional or physical pain.

What I have chosen to believe is this. Being molested catapulted me into an amazing journey that was sometimes painful, but ultimately it caused me to explore my sense of self. As a result I am able to share my new found wisdom with my clients, the people I teach, and with you, so that we can all live fuller, richer lives. It catapulted me into an exploration that allowed me to claim my 'divine sexual self' and share that with a loving and passionate mate. I am in no way saying that what happened was right. I would not wish it to happen to anyone else but I know that I am the person that I am in some respects because of it.

I have taken the gift from the experience, and allowed that to shape me, instead of getting caught up in what I could perceive to be mistakes, "Why didn't I check that the door was locked?", "I shouldn't have done anything that might have drawn attention to me", etc. I know this might be quite a leap of faith for some of you. But think for a moment about some of the big events in your life. See how you reacted to them. Did you do the best that you could have done, given your circumstances at the time?

It doesn't matter that you would do things differently now. You are a different person now to the person that you were then, even if then was two minutes or two years ago. Knowing what you know now, how can you use this experience to make a positive impact on your life? It might be that you take a class, join a support group, reach out and help someone in the same circumstance. Once you use the experience to extend out of yourself so that you can grow, you will be amazed to see the avenues of opportunity and learning that present themselves to you.

Part of the nature being a Taurean is that I can be quite stubborn. Years ago, if I made my mind up about something, that was it. There was no way I was changing my opinion, or going back on my word. Over time I discovered how limiting this was, and I developed the awareness that defending an old belief did not sit well in my body. When I would stick to my guns to argue an old point, I would feel like a jig saw that was all jumbled up. I felt uncomfortable in my skin.

Now, if I'm talking to someone I will often say that this is my opinion now, but I might feel differently in a week or in a month. It gives me license to change my mind, but it also allows me to be more honest with people, and to be open to new ideas. It is so freeing, and it releases me from my own dogmatic thought patterns. Similarly I have let go of the belief that because I am a Taurean I have to be stubborn. Instead I see it as something I can choose to believe in, and align to, or not.

So for now just accept that you are the sum of all the parts of your life. Life has made you who you are, and because of the experiences you've had, you are in fact perfect. How you choose to live your life based on the experiences you've had, and the wisdom you acquire each and every day is up to you. The good news is that you can make new choices every moment.

The ability to choose is a delicious experiment, whereby you are sensing the awareness that vibrates in your body. It is an awareness that vibrates with each new, and sometimes old repetitive choice. How does each choice feel in the very core of your being? Does it make you feel nervous but good? Does it make you feel claustrophobic? Is it exhilarating? Or does it feel constraining? Do you feel guilty, or do you feel more like yourself? Start small if you like. Try by choosing a different type of coffee or muffin the next time you are in a coffee shop, and track your awareness as it works its way through your body.

As women, one of the areas in which we so desperately lack self appreciation is in relation to our bodies. The female form, both internally and externally, is a masterpiece of creation. Yet if you take a straw poll of the women you know and ask how many of them love and appreciate their bodies, I'm guessing the positive responses will be low. You might get a lot of "Mmmm … I guess I do. I'm just not crazy about my thighs/bum/breasts/nose, etc."

Our body is an amazing gift. It allows us to experience life. We can run, walk, jump, sing, dance, smell, taste and touch because we have a body. Without you having to consciously think about it, your body breathes, excretes and digests for you. Because of it, we can hold a new baby, pick a flower, and caress a lover. We can experience what it is to cry and to laugh. How many times have you heard people say that they did not appreciate their body until an accident disabled some part of it? Yet this doesn't tend to make us think any differently about our own bodies, or treat them any better. Instead, we wile away the hours thinking about all the bits, and that's what we call them; 'bits' of our bodies that we don't like.

Exercise – Healing your relationship with your Body

- Take a moment, and take a few deep breaths.
- Now starting at your feet bring your awareness to each part of your body.
- Your feet, legs, thigh, pelvis etc. working your through every part of your body. Pay special attention to the 'bits' you don't particularly like.
- Now tell each part of your body that you are grateful to it and why.
- So for example "Feet, I am so grateful that you take me on my morning walk through the forest."
- "Legs, I am so grateful that because of you I get to wear my favourite jeans. Hips, I am so grateful that because of you I can go dancing, etc."
- Find gratitude, no matter how small or seemingly ridiculous, for each part of your body.
- Now tomorrow and everyday thereafter when you are in the shower or putting on your body lotion afterwards, tell each part of your body as you are massaging it with shower gel or lotion why you are grateful to it.
- This is a very simple exercise but I promise you, if you do it every day for 28 days, the effect on how you feel about yourself will be profound.

Exercise – The Miracle of the Female Form

- The female form is a work of art. Artists, sculptures, poets and writers have tried to convey the beauty of the female body since the beginning of time. She (being woman) is mysterious, mystical and magical. Let go of any negative feelings you have regarding the female body for a moment and journey with me.

- In your minds eye call up the image of the archetypal feminine, that curvy figure that represents womanhood.

- From the objectiveness of the observer, look at her body.

- Look into her eyes, which are the windows of her soul, and taste the juiciness of her lips.

- See how her neck curls down to her shoulder like chocolate shavings, guiding you to the litheness of her arms and her fingertips, eager to caress.

- Allow your eyes to bask in the beauty of the orbs of nurturing and pleasure that are her breasts, before allowing your gaze to travel to her navel. The navel is that lineage chord that connects her to her mother, and to her mother's mother, and to each and every woman that has gone before her.

- Massage her belly with your gaze, that beautiful mound of creative potential that embraces all new life.

- Watch as the outline of her body gently expands from the camber of her waist to the sensual curve of her hips.
- The hips hugging the pelvic girdle are the home of her womanly fire.
- Dancing delicately at the centre of her pelvis is the entrance to her vagina, teasing, inviting, longing.
- This is passageway to her fire, her most sacred site.
- All of this beautiful architecture is like natures rolling hills, and is supported by her legs.
- Each day these legs carry her further into the garden.
- As she stands firmly on her feet, her toes are tantalised by the feel of mother earth on her skin.
- Her body is a delicious symphony of curves; her calves, her thighs, her hips, the small of her back, her belly, her breasts, her neck and her lips.
- In every aspect of her being her body mirrors the kundalini, the sacred coiling serpent-like energy of sexuality and creation.
- What a miracle she is to behold.

So what do we do with this divine miracle? Do we honour her? Do we treat her with reverence and love? For most of us the answer to this question is an unequivocal "No." We are created in the image and likeness of God. This is not news. Most of us have heard this from the time we were children. Yet do we believe it? The feminine form is the feminine energy of God, given physical shape. God in his/her wisdom, loved us so much that he/she gave us this beautiful body so that we could experience the essence and energy of the godlike feminine. The same is true for men in relation to experiencing the masculine.

We have this wonderful divine body and what do we do with it. We starve it or overfeed it. We try to change its shape. We bitch that its shape is not the same as the shapes on the front of those glossy magazines that have airbrushed all traces of true femininity away. We tell ourselves that we are too fat or too thin; that we have too little cleavage, or too much. We cover our bodies in baggy clothes because we are ashamed of them, or march them off to a doctors surgery, so that he can cut out or suck out the 'bits' we don't like. God gave us this miracle, this divine creation, and we torture it in so many ways, like a vile traitor that we have discovered in our midst.

Exercise – Bridging the Gap

- Take a breath.
- Ask the following question to your heart, not your mind, and go with the first number that you get: To what extent (out of 100) do you honestly love your body?

- The extent to which you love your body is one indication of the extent to which you love yourself.
- Do not be hard on yourself if the number is low. Just be aware that there is plenty of room for improvement.

Your body is the temple of your inner garden. It is the vessel which contains the moist luscious essence of womanhood. If you do not tend to it, and love it, your garden will perish. Your body is the container where those seeds of womanhood start to grow. It is impossible to separate them. You cannot come into union with your womanhood if you are not willing to come into union with your body. Ask yourself:

- Are you willing to leave all the old negative programming and beliefs about your body behind?
- Are you instead willing to accept that, no matter what shape you are, whatever your physical health, or sexual orientation, that your body is the divine energy of the feminine God made manifest?

Like each flower, your body is unique. In being unique it represents its own distinctive aspect of the Divine Feminine. If the answer is yes, even if it is a tentative somewhat nervous yes, then come with me. We are going to go a little deeper into your garden.

Where we venture next on our journey together is the

most sacred of all hallowed ground. It is our birthright, and yet only a few brave and curious souls have travelled there. We resist navigating the territory and investigating the terrain, and in doing so we deprive ourselves of the most essential gift of womanhood: the gift of connecting to the source of our feminine power.

- Where is this holy land?
- Why do we choose not to go there?
- How can travelling to this hidden place infuse us with the energy of our radiance?

Exercise – Meeting our Inner Landscape

- If you wish to discover the location of this ancient land, sit with your feet on the floor, place your hands gently on your knees, and take a few deep breaths.
- Now very gently and very slowly start to draw your hands up along your inner thighs.
- Keep going until the fingertips on both hands meet and come to rest on your pubic bone. This is the entrance to your 'holy land.'
- Congratulations, you have just taken those first tentative steps to a land where few have dared to go.
- How did that feel?
- Was it easy, or was there resistance?
- Did you feel like a naughty school girl, afraid of being

caught, or did it feel natural and easy?
- Just be aware, there is no right and no wrong way to do this. It's simply an exercise in observation.

Your energetic centre of female power has many names; pussy, vagina, gee, minge, cunt or down there are but a few. Personally, I dislike vagina for two reasons. Firstly, it sounds so cold and disassociated. For me it bears no energetic connection to the wonderment of what it is trying to describe. Secondly, vagina means 'sheath for a sword', and for me I believe it is so much more. Also, the vagina is merely the passageway from the external sexual organs to the cervix and the womb; the term when used to describe a woman's sexual organs is incomplete. Instead, I personally prefer the ancient Sanskrit word for the female genitals, which is Yoni, meaning 'sacred place.'

I realise that for many of you the thought of having to go 'down there' strikes the fear of God into you. But please, do not abandon this journey just yet. Your yoni contains all the wisdom of your womanhood. It is the home of your internal fire. It is the resting place for your divine energy, which causes your seeds to grow, and your garden to blossom. We shall journey gently so that you can remember, and reconnect, with the beauty of who you are.

One of the gifts of womanhood is the gift of creation. Conception is the divine union of masculine and feminine to create new life. Our bodies feed and nurture that new life until it is ready to be birthed into the world. As woman we embody the gift of life. What a precious miracle that is. It does not matter if you do not want children, or if you are past child bearing age. Try to honour that gift of the potentiality, the divine miracle that can take place in your body.

I realise that for many women this is a sensitive subject. If you are unable to get pregnant, if you have miscarried or if you have terminated a pregnancy, being a vessel for life may seem like a cruel and heartless jibe. This is not my intention. The ability to birth life is a huge aspect of womanhood. Your personal relationship with this aspect of your femininity is a huge part of your journey in life.

My husband and I tried for approximately two years to try and get pregnant. I spent each month waiting to see if I would escape the knowing twitch in my lower back that would signal the onset of my period. But each month my body cleansed and released its blood. This was followed by the immediate wave of disappointment that was suppressed so that I could dust myself off and start again anew.

The months went by. Eventually I went back to my doctor who had assured me early on in the process that "It just takes time, the best thing to do is forget about it and go on with your life." Almost another two years later she agreed that trying to 'forget about it' wasn't working, and she sent me for tests. After much undignified poking and prodding I was sent for a laparoscopy, which revealed that I had endometriosis. With endometriosis the endometrial tissue, which is responsible for your menstrual cycle, grows in other areas of your pelvis instead of remaining within the uterus. This can cause very painful periods, which I had all my life, and can be a factor in infertility.

I suppose I should have been relieved. At least I had an explanation. Instead, I was furious with God. Energetically, endometriosis is blocked energy in your second chakra. Your second chakra is the cosmic energy centre that is located for women in their womb. In energy medicine, if you are holding an issue in your chakra that it is left unprocessed, which then festers, it will eventually show up in your physical body, demanding your attention so that it can be healed. There are many issues that can affect your second chakra, including lack of self worth, low self esteem, insecurity with regard to money, and not owning your talents.

One other big issue that affects this chakra is sexual abuse of any kind.

I was livid. As far as I was concerned I had done my healing work with regard to being molested, and yet the rot had taken a firm hold in my body. How could God do this to me? I had done all that had been asked of me.

I had become the psychic. I was doing God's work, and in the process healing my stuff. Then when I had asked for this one thing, a baby, I had been dealt this cruel and sneaky blow.

As a result of the laparoscopy I had laser surgery to remove the growth. When I was discharged I left the hospital tired and sore, but the greatest pain lingered in my heart. The next few days were muddled; a mixture of raw emotion and the after effects of the anaesthetic. I had never had an anaesthetic before, and I share this experience with you now, because at the time I had absolutely no idea what was happening to me. You in turn might find it useful if it ever happens to you.

After several days when I was supposed to be 'back on my feet' I was still spaced. I felt like part of me was separate from my body, and that I couldn't get back in. It was like being in a dream state, or an out of body experience, but it lasted all day and through the night. Thankfully Enid came to my rescue. As I lay on her plinth she started to massage me with cold marble stones, and something magical started to happen. I could feel the cold of the stones shocking my cells awake. Bit by bit, as she massaged me I began to feel the haze lifting. By the time I got off the plinth I was back in my body and feeling alive again.

On returning to the doctors surgery for my check up, she informed me that they (the medical profession) didn't really know what caused endometrioses, or how to stop it coming back. If it did come back they would simply do another laparoscopy. In that instant I promised myself I would never go through that experience again. I know doctors do amazing work, and I believe that if you are in a road traffic accident for example, and if you are losing blood, the best place in the world to be is the A&E department of a hospital. You can be the most highly ascended being on the planet but it would take some amount of chanting for you to reattach a severed limb. Having said that, Western medicine is mostly reactionary. It is reacting to something that has already happened in the body; a trauma, a fever, or an irregular cell growth.

In ancient Taoist China, you paid the doctor when you were well because it was his job to make sure that you stayed well. If you got sick you stopped paying him because he had failed at his job. How different would our healthcare systems be if we took that approach? Complementary and integrative health is making strides to empower each person to take responsibility for their well being. Practitioners are working with clients to keep them well, as opposed to waiting until they get sick. If the Titanic had changed her course by 1 degree earlier on in her voyage, the cumulative effect would have meant that she would never have hit that iceberg. How many of us fail to change our course by that 1 degree, and instead wait until we have our own collision. Then we decide to do something.

With this in mind I decided to take responsibility for my body, and for my wellness. I have often fought with God. Like an angry five year old I will throw a tantrum and stamp my feet until my face turns blue. When the temper subsides however, every child wants to be held in the loving arms of their parent. And so it is with me.

When the anger abated, and the tears and frustration subsided, I returned to the loving arms of God and I prayed. I prayed for help; for someone to help me heal my body so that I would be able to conceive. My angel appeared in the form of a friend of mine. She told me about a clinic in Dublin that was doing wonderful work with all sorts of ailments, using a combination of acupuncture, organ cleanses, herbs and supplements.

When I went along for a consultation I immediately knew I was in the right place. The consultant asked me about my periods, and within moments he had joined together all the pieces of a puzzle that had niggled at me for years; the excruciating pain, the diarrhoea at the start of each period, and the clotting, etc. He explained why it all happened and how he could help me address the problem. Years before, when I had visited the doctor with these symptoms, his solution had been to prescribe for me the contraceptive pill.

I embarked on a new journey; a process of

systematically cleansing each organ in my body. I helped my body rid itself of toxins, and built it up with herbs and supplements. Initially, I had acupuncture and Chinese cupping three times a week to help my body offset its toxic load. I was gradually weaned to one acupuncture treatment a week as my body got stronger. There were enemas, fasting, juices and healing crises. I watched in amazement as waves of anger washed through my body as I cleansed my liver. I watched in awe as my physical shape changed. I was embraced by wonderment as the thick dark blood and clots of my menstrual cycle were replaced by a beautiful ruby red flow. My skin glowed, my hair was shiny, my nails grew strong, and I felt and looked amazing.

For the first time in my life, I knew my body intimately. I understood how she worked, what she needed, and what she liked and didn't like. I was awe struck by her ability to heal, given the right conditions, and I felt blessed. I felt blessed that even though difficult circumstances had brought me to this point I had in fact been given such a gift. For the first time in my life I understood what it was to have a woman's body, and how it worked. It was, and still is, an amazing feeling. It connected me with what seemed like a voice that had been living inside for so very long, and now, at last, its wisdom had a chance to be heard.

Exercise – Journeying to your Sacred Place

This is a beautiful exercise which will help you connect to your core. Take some time to do it when you won't be disturbed and where you can enjoy the process.

- Sit or lie comfortably.
- Close your eyes and take some nice deep centring breaths.
- Place one hand on your lower belly, and one hand, if you can reach it, on the small of your back, so that your sacred centre, your womb, and reproductive organs are being held gently and lovingly between both hands.
- Take some time to breathe into this lower part of your belly, allowing your hands to rise and fall with the breath.
- As you breathe, engage your imagination and allow your awareness to travel into the landscape of your sacred place.
- Like an adventurer explore this new landscape with your minds eye.
- Are there rivers, mountains or valleys, or does it look like a dark cave, or outer space?
- You may wish to imagine that you are in a submarine exploring these hidden depths. Whatever you sense or see is perfect.

- For most of you this will be your first visit here so be patient and gentle with yourself.
- With childlike wonderment explore your surroundings, especially the areas that may be hidden around a corner, or down a tunnel, or over a hill.
- As you explore this place get a sense of how you feel about it.
- What is your relationship with it?
- Is it one of fear, repulsion or loathing?
- Is it one of unfamiliarity and disappointment?
- Is it one of love and connection?
- Don't judge yourself. Remember, this is merely a journey of exploration.
- When you are ready, visualise yourself standing or sitting in the centre of this inner landscape, and say out loud three times, so that every cell in your body hears you, "I love and appreciate myself exactly as I am."
- When you are ready takes some breaths and bring your awareness back into the room.
- When you are ready record your experiences, without judging yourself, in your notebook.

The Third Stepping Stone
∼ Forgiveness ∼

"*To move forward, to heal, we must first forgive. Forgiveness is one of the quintessential components of our healing process, as it allows us to let go of the past. Forgiveness is not easy, and must not be done from a place of force, or "I have to forgive, so that I can move forward." Forgiveness is gentle, and yet powerful. You must forgive from that gentle vulnerable place inside you. Forgiveness from the place of the warrior is not forgiveness. What you are doing is saying the other person was wrong, but you are high and mighty enough to let bygones be bygones. This is faux forgiveness. Forgiveness must come from your heart. There is no blame, no retribution required, just a willingness to let go and honour the experience.*"

I must say that for me personally I have really struggled with forgiveness. Entering the forgiveness process did not come easily to me. When I was hurt, and mad, and had recoiled from life like a dog licking at her wounds, the last thing in the world I wanted to do was forgive. Usually I wanted blood. I wanted to inflict as much pain and suffering on the person who had hurt me as humanly possible. I wanted them to die squirming, feeling my pain a thousand fold, knowing the trauma they had caused, while vowing never to do it again.

Ironically, I seldom lashed out at my supposed perpetrator. Instead I withdrew. I withdrew into myself, refusing to talk, smarting from the hurt, planning out revenge scenarios in my mind. All the time I became moodier and bitter. Fortunately for them, and for myself, I have realised that this approach doesn't work. When you inflict pain on someone, no matter how much you perceive that they have hurt you, revenge never ever soothes the pain. You may disagree, but I ask you to honestly ask yourself: if you have ever committed an act of revenge, and withdrawal is an act of revenge, did it really make your pain go away, in the long term? It may have given you some temporary relief, but I'm betting that after the adrenalin abated the pain was right there, waiting for you again.

I think there are many challenges in life, but I believe the two greatest challenges we face as human beings are firstly to forgive, and secondly to love. The irony is that they are intertwined, and one can not normally exist without the presence of the other. For love to enter into a situation we often have to forgive ourselves, or another person, and without forgiveness the doorway to love always remains shut.

You may say "Well, I love my kids. There is no need to forgive them", and that's a valid point. But how many times have your kids done something to upset, annoy, or frustrate you? Yes, you still love them, but in doing so you've had to let go of the times where you didn't feel a whole lot of love towards them. This is called forgiveness, and it's a two way street. You have to forgive them for doing something that upset you, and you have to forgive yourself for feeling upset. It's okay to be upset. In fact, it is healthy.

Therapists consulting rooms are full of people who have spent years suppressing their feelings. Finally they erupt in a sometimes dangerous, or harmful, way. When we don't allow ourselves to feel, whether it is what we perceive to be a positive or negative emotion, we restrict the flow of energy through our bodies, and we stagnate.

Feeling is incredibly important. I spent many years almost numb, denying my feelings. When I opened the floodgates the avalanche of emotion that poured through sometimes overwhelmed me. I could only feel when pushed to the extremes of emotion. If something was incredibly sad I would cry. If it was hilariously funny I would laugh, but I kept the middle ground of the emotional spectrum under lock and key, so there was no danger of any hurt seeping through. Sadly when you go to such extremes to block out the pain, the joy gets blocked out too.

Consider this for a moment. Imagine that between you and everyone you know there is a hollow pipe from your heart to theirs. What flows through this pipe is unconditional love, and the flow goes both ways. Every time you experience a negative thought or emotion towards the person your pipe is connected to, your pipe contracts, reducing its size, and in doing so it reduces the amount of love that can flow through the pipe. Every time the person at the other end of the pipe has a negative thought or emotion towards you the pipe contracts. Over time the pipe between two people gets so constricted that there is actually no room for love to flow between them.

This is often the case in marriages or romantic relationships. They start out with the open pipe, and over time each little thing that either partner does or says that appears hurtful to the other eventually causes the pipe to narrow. One day you wake up beside that person, wondering how in the world you ever loved them in the first place. In many cases we don't even start a relationship with an open pipe. Past experiences that we carry with us into the present limit our willingness to open the pipe, so that we avoid being hurt again.

Frequently, when we start a new relationship, we start from a limited capacity. We enter into a relationship with an armour plated pipe, where we control the flow, because we will be damned if this person (boss, lover, sibling) is going to hurt you like you were hurt before. This is why forgiveness is so important. When you forgive both yourself and others you reopen the pipe. In opening the pipe you increase your vitality, your life force energy, and you are, once again, available for life.

I can hear you asking, "Why do I need to forgive myself, and why should I forgive them? They were really hurtful, abusive, nasty, insincere, etc." This is a fair question. You must firstly forgive yourself for judging the other person, and for making the assumption that they were trying to hurt you, and maybe they were. In Don Miguel Ruiz's book *The Four Agreements*, one of the agreements states, "Don't take anything personally." I struggled with this concept because it goes on to say, "Don't take anything personally, positive or negative." Yet I have found this simple teaching to be incredibly profound. You are Divine energy made manifest, ergo you are the Divine. The Divine cannot be created or destroyed. It just 'is'. What can be destroyed or broken is the human ego. If you are Divine, you are perfection. If you take something somebody says or does to you personally, and allow it to have an effect on you, you are allowing it to have an effect on the ego mind.

We allow our interactions with other people to either plump up or deflate our ego. There are volumes and volumes of texts written on the ego. Many of them, especially the spiritual texts, talk about containing, or reducing, the power of the ego so that we do not live our lives as slaves to it. This is valid discourse, however, if the ego is such a pain in the ass, why on earth have we got one? The ego is an aspect of God made manifest. It is the shadow aspect of God.

For every thing in the universe there must be a polar opposite. For night there must be day. For love there must be hate, and for joy their must be sadness. The ego allows us to experience the Divine within ourselves. In stepping away from the Divine and allowing ourselves to fall away from that place of grace within, we have the opportunity to journey back to the Divine. Then we can realise our beauty, and reacquaint ourselves with our grace.

This may seem terribly complicated, and in some ways I think it is, but for a moment think about something beautiful in your life. It might be someone special. It might be a picture hanging on a wall of your home, or it might be a beautiful manifestation of nature that you pass on your way to work, or the grocery store. How often during the day do you stop to appreciate it?

Is it often the case that you take it for granted, and don't truly *see* it there. I notice this with paintings in my home. I chose them because they were beautiful and something about them caught my attention. Yet I often notice that I don't really notice them. I see the frame hanging on the wall, but weeks can go by without me actually seeing what is contained within the frame.

How often in life do we do this on a daily basis? You may see your children, or your co-workers, or your mate on a daily basis, but how often do you actually *see* them, and honour their presence. Then, as is often the case in life where something happens and they are no longer in our lives, we feel guilty for not seeing and appreciating them when they were present. Communities may take their park area for granted, and only realise its beauty when a developer wants to remove it to build more houses. We don't realise the beauty in having fresh water to drink until something pollutes our water supply. So in every aspect of life, we take that which is beautiful and present for granted.

This is the case with the Divine. It is ever present, but to appreciate it, we have to lose it, so that we can come back to it. This is the job of the ego. The ego separates us from the Divine. It's a worthwhile job in the grand cosmic scheme of things, because if we didn't have it, we wouldn't get to experience the miracle that is life. Somewhere, however, this grand plan has gone wrong. For whatever reason (and I don't have the answer to this one) humanity has decided, albeit unconsciously, to dwell in the realm of the ego.

Think of both the ego and the Divine as an oscillating pulse. We alternate between both energies. It is like swinging from shadow to light. In doing this we get to appreciate the nuances and aspects of both. We feel the coldness of the seclusion of the shadow. Then we can appreciate the warmth and inclusiveness of the light. The ego was never designed to be a permanent state, yet this is where most of us live our lives, from the depths of the shadows.

When we allow someone's comments or actions, either positive or negative, to shape how we are feeling, we are operating from the realm of the ego. This is okay. Once we bring our awareness to it, it allows us to forgive ourselves for being led by the ego. This opens the pipe to love, and allows us to rest once again in the Divine. And so the dance continues. Similarly, when we forgive the person involved, not from a place judgement, but from a position of awareness, we once again open the pipe to love.

By now I'm sure you are wondering what all this ego forgiveness stuff has to do with tending to your inner garden. I'm glad you asked. There is a saying, "As within so without." Roughly translated, this means whatever is happening to you internally is reflected in your external world. If there is hate or fear within, you will see it in many aspects of your everyday life. Similarly, if there is love and compassion within, this will be reflected back to you.

While I admit that I have said that the universe is a union of opposites, something seems to be out of balance in our world. Fear, hate, war, and famine have somehow managed to tip the scales in their favour. Many people feel like prey; being constantly stalked by an invisible predator. The world for many people does not feel like a safe and loving place.

Forgiveness, love and compassion are not exclusively, but are predominantly, feminine traits. As women, if we can learn to forgive, and have compassion for ourselves, this will be reflected in our world. As women, we need to open the pipe; firstly to ourselves, and then to the world at large. Imagine the difference that this could make to our world. For a moment imagine that you forgave yourself for every perceived wrong doing in your life. Imagine that you opened the pipe to yourself so wide that every cell in your body radiated unconditional love and forgiveness.

This is not to say that you will never oscillate into shadow, but once you do, your awareness catches it. You can then use forgiveness as your leverage to bring you back into the light. Now imagine if you extended that pipe to everyone you knew. As you open it, it causes a simultaneous reflex. This allows them not only to open their pipe back to you, but to everyone they know. In doing so, you start a domino effect, which ripples out across the world. Let your mind go wild, and imagine that, if everyone on the planet connected to the love within (and therefore the Divine), we would no longer act out from a place of shadow and wounding.

I am asking you to take a leap of faith. Imagine that if you loved yourself completely that you wouldn't hurt your children, your friends, or your colleagues. If you didn't hurt the people in your life on an emotional, physical or psychological level, they would not have to act out from their woundings (i.e. their ego self) towards others. Take one minute to imagine the ripple effect this would have. Instead of living in a world of fear we would live in a world of balance, and love. This does not mean that what we perceive as bad things won't happen. Remember, the world oscillates between shadow and light. Instead of using our current world method of fighting fear with fear, and hate with hate, we can melt away fear and hate with love and forgiveness, and once again return to balance.

I realise that for many of you this may seem incredibly simplistic, but in reality it is not. It takes great inner strength and courage to forgive; much more so than to initiate an act of war. In forgiveness we are vulnerable, and we are choosing to relinquish outcome.

When we lash out at someone we are looking in some way for payback. When we forgive, we are opening the door for balance and love to enter, in whatever form it may take. What we perceive as balance may not be the intention of the universe. We must forgive with an open and willing heart, with no expectation of what will follow.

One thing I must stress; I am not saying that if you or somebody you love is in an abusive or dangerous situation, that all you must do is channel forgiveness. Firstly remove yourself, or your loved one, from the situation, and then as part of the healing process, embrace the energy of forgiveness.

How many people in your life do you know who are still angry or hurt over something that happened in the past? Their anger and bitterness is often palpable, and in many cases it contorts and atrophies their body. Once your energy is stuck in the past, you are not available for the present. You are not available for life.

In the garden, once a season has past, it is past. We let it go, and enjoy the blessings and beauty that the new season brings with it. There will be another summer, and winter, but it will never be exactly the same as the one that came before. We cannot enjoy the new unfolding energy if we are clinging to what was, or could have been. Forgiveness frees us from the past. It is the catalyst that allows us to move forward; to grow and experience. Are you stuck in a repetitive cycle of hurt and frustration? Do you want to stay there for the rest of your life, languishing in the shadows, or do you want let go of the old, and make way for something delicious and new? If so, it is time to make space for forgiveness in your life.

Exercise — Opening the Pipe

This is a really beautiful exercise, and while it appears remarkably simple, I have found it to have incredible results. All you need is a willingness to let go. Initially, you can set aside some time and space to practice it, but over time you will be able to do it with your eyes open; on the bus, in your car, or standing in line in the canteen.

- Sit or lie comfortably.
- Take a few deep centring breaths and close your eyes.
- With your eyes closed imagine someone standing about six feet away from you, with whom you are out of balance. You either feel that you have hurt them, or that they have hurt you.
- Now imagine a pipe about eight inches in diameter connecting your heart to theirs.
- As you breathe, with each exhale, allow the energy of forgiveness to travel down the pipe towards their heart.
- With each inhale allow the energy of forgiveness to

travel up the pipe, from them to you.

- If you find it difficult to connect with the energy of forgiveness you can visualise healing white light travelling down the pipe as you exhale, and up the pipe as you inhale. Alternatively, you can say the word forgiveness after each breath.

- Continue to breathe, allowing the energy of forgiveness to travel up and down the pipe. Remember, you are connecting your Divine heart energy to their Divine heart energy, so they may appear different in your visualisation than they do in your everyday life.

- Be open to being surprised as to what can happen when you connect, essence to essence, with someone, as opposed to ego to ego.

- When you feel that it is appropriate and that the energy of forgiveness has cleared and expanded the pipe between both of you, allow the energy of unconditional love to flow down the pipe as you exhale, and travel up the pipe to you from the person you are visualising as you inhale.

- Again, if you have difficulty connecting to the energy of unconditional love, visualise healing pink light travelling up and down the pipe, or say the word love after each breath.

- Be gentle with yourself. It may take several attempts at this exercise before you reach a stage where you can send and receive love.

- When you feel that the exchange is complete, allow the pipe to evaporate, knowing that the love and forgiveness connection remains.
- Take a few grounding breaths, and gently open your eyes.
- Repeat this process over time for everyone you need to come into balance with, including yourself, friends, family, clients, people who have hurt you, and world leaders.

This exercise can also be done with someone who has passed away, or with a baby that is in utero.

The Fourth Stepping Stone
～ *Love* ～

"*When we forgive, we clear the energy between two people. This is a beautiful healing and joining of souls, but it is not complete. Divine energy does not respond to forgiveness. This is something that has been designed to facilitate us mortals in our healing process. Divine energy vibrates to the frequency of love. If you want to bring the Divine into every situation and relationship in your life, you must do so in the presence of love. You think that you can't love someone who has hurt you. This is not true. This is the ego trying to sabotage you from aligning to your Divine energy, the true Self.*

Love is incandescent luminosity. Try to imagine if every moment of your day was filled with the radiant light of love. Imagine how

164

you would live, engage with people, rear your children. Imagine how the world would be different; how wars would cease. And yet fear and hate prevails. We are so afraid of our capacity to love that we sabotage ourselves at every given opportunity. To be in love means to be in your truth, your vulnerability, and your wholeness. Yet most of us do not want to present ourselves, in this naked humble way, to the world. So we manufacture scenarios where we can pretend to be something else, to hide our beauty, so that we can keep hidden from the world.

Do you think a warring soldier is showing his beauty? No, he is showing his rage. Do you think a mother who hits her child is connected to Divine source? No, she is connected to infinite pain. And yet these are choices we make. To move forward you must ask yourself, are you willing to choose love and be that radiant light?"

I really struggled with this chapter. Initially, I felt like it was a repetition of the previous one. I sat and poured over the opening paragraph, stuck and unable to write. I wandered the gardens of my idyllic oasis, searching for a way through my apparent impasse. I lingered amongst the radiant tapestry of autumnal colours which surrounded me, ever expectant of a Divine spark of wisdom to break through. I have prayed, explored and even drank cappuccinos; my pen constantly at the ready to catch the wave of inspiration as soon as it sailed through, and yet nothing.

Finally, overwhelmed by frustration, I called my sage

like partner to discuss my conundrum, in the hope that he could shed some light on this apparently elusive subject. The call was a complete success, not because he provided the solution to my dilemma, but because he provoked me into a furious rage, which eventually crumbled a mental and emotional barricade. Then I became open to a new and deeper understanding of Love.

After fifteen years of being together, and four years of trying to get pregnant, cracks began to appear in my marriage. The cracks had possibly been there for quite some time, but now, for whatever reason, they made their way to the surface. What followed was an incredibly painful period of counselling and soul searching, after which my husband and I decided to separate. I don't believe that there is anything to be gained by lingering on the details, other than to say I think we both felt that we had been ripped to our core. We were catapulted into a whirlwind of disbelief. "This was something that happened to other people. Surely it couldn't be happening to us." We were, as everyone pointed out, the 'perfect couple'. But it *was* happening, and when the whirlwind settled, the stark reality of our situation sunk in. It was like being in a nightmare, but you were all the time expecting to wake up. It wasn't a dream. These nightmarish events had somehow become our reality.

Over the years I gave spiritual readings to several women, for whom the advice has been to end their relationship. I would gaze in wonderment at them when they would return months later, and still be in the same relationship. They had received guidance; why did they not follow it through? Only now, after undertaking this journey myself, do I understand how completely arrogant I was. There is an old saying, "To understand someone, walk a mile in their shoes." Only after walking the path of separation myself do I realise what a soul wrenching, heart breaking experience it is. I truly understand why many women choose to stay in a relationship, no matter how unhappy or unfulfilled they may feel, instead of walking a solitary path. With complete humility, I apologise to any of those women that I judged. I was arrogant and unkind. Please forgive me.

After my separation, an intensely dark and challenging period followed, where I was forced to take a long hard look at myself. If I am to be completely honest I must admit that I didn't particularly like, never mind love, the person that I saw. The person that I saw was selfish, inconsiderate and unrelenting. She wanted life on her terms, and was inconsolable when this didn't occur. What I see now is how much of my life had been based on fear and control. If I could control my life, and everything in it, there was no need to be fearful. Then I could be happy. This might have worked, except that happiness cannot exist in the presence of control, as happiness in its essence is uncontrollable. Happiness is like a breeze, you cannot tell from where it originated or where it will end its course. It may feel like a warm caress, a spine tingling tickle, or a breath-taking gust. But the second you try to catch the breeze, all that remains are palms full of stagnant air, and you have ceased to enjoy the experience.

There are many words that I could use to describe how I felt at this time, but happy was definitely not one of them. I was exhausted, melancholy, miserable, deflated, emotionally battered, and bruised, but the words that I kept returning to time and time again were 'unloving' and 'unlovable'. I felt that I was unable to give love, and unable to feel love. Over the following months as I rode the rollercoaster of daily emotions that presented themselves, one of the few things that I was certain about, was that, whether or not I was able to love someone else, or be loved by someone else, I sure as hell didn't love myself.

I felt ugly from the inside out. I had vowed to this lovely man to spend the rest of our lives together, and I hated myself for breaking that promise. I felt that I lacked integrity; that I had shattered his dreams, and disappointed my family. Why could I not have shut up and put up? The reason I can see now, as I retrace my steps, is simple. Unknown to myself, I was tentatively stepping out into the garden, and placing one foot in front of the other on the stepping stones of life. I was following the healing process outlined in this book, before the seeds of this book had ever been sown. I was being asked to walk the walk, before I was guided to talk the talk. My awareness had finally gotten my attention and made me take a closer look at my marriage.

As I entered the energy of self appreciation I realised that, within the confines of my marriage, I was dying. My soul essence, that longed to express herself in her totality, was suffocating, and feeling ever more lost and listless as time continued. And so I entered the process of forgiveness. I had to forgive myself for all the negative thoughts, feelings and emotions I had about myself. I had to forgive my husband for all the perceived wrong doings that I had blamed him for. When I finally purged myself of my anger, fear and self loathing, something new began to fill the empty space. That something new was love.

I came to realise that I was perfection in my imperfection. God had created me in his image and likeness, so even my perceived imperfections were aspects of the Divine. Over time I came to firstly accept, and then love, myself. I learned to love myself for simply being me. I had to let go of all the masks I presented to the world and all the judgements I made upon myself. When I stripped away all the layers I felt naked and vulnerable inside. If I wasn't wife, lover, teacher, therapist, friend, daughter and sister, who or what was I, and what was there to love?

What I discovered instead, as I rested in my new found vulnerability, was a spark; a tiny spark of Divine essence that had been buried deep within. It didn't have to do anything to prove itself; or to get, find, or give love. It was just love. What I came to realise was that it was the spark that others saw in me, and yet I had been unable to recognise it in myself. My friends and family didn't want to hang out with me because of what I did, or because of what I was, but because they loved being in the presence of that Divine spark, the same way that I enjoyed being in the presence of theirs. I realised how many times I had been with people, and it was enough to simply be in their company. They didn't have to do or say or prove anything.

Think of someone you know who is, to use that old expression, 'comfortable in their skin'. There is no effort involved for them in being who they are, and they are always a pleasure to be around. Whether they know it or not, the reason they are comfortable in their skin is because they have reached a place of self acceptance within themselves. In doing so they have also embraced self love. They are the Divine; that spark of life force energy made manifest, and they are perfect.

Amidst the chaos and trauma of my soul searching, I became involved in a new romantic relationship. Initially, I resisted it like the plague. I even employed some heavy duty shamanic techniques in an attempt to drive him away.

This succeeded in giving him what felt like a bad hangover, but he remained undeterred. I felt that the relationship was inappropriate. I was confused and raw, and yet part of me was exhilarated. My ego was flattered. As I reflect on this time I wonder what he ever saw in me. I was an emotional wreck. I could berate myself and say that I entered into this relationship insincerely, as emotionally I had little to give. In my heart however, I feel that this relationship was Divinely timed. It was the catalyst that transitioned me into a new chapter of my life.

He and I had met several years previously. He had come to me for a reading at a very difficult point in his life. In truth, I was not in the habit of sizing up my male clients, but I remember looking at him and thinking, "This man is a train wreck. There is no way I could ever fancy him." I'm sure that the universe must have laughed heartily that day. I'm not really sure how, but over the years he ceased to be my client, and we eventually became friends.

What brought us together, however, was our mutual desire to teach a Medicine Wheel. He had studied the North American tradition of the wheel, and I was a student of the South American model. When two wilful and idealistic people come together to work on a project, there is bound to be some tension. After many labour pains, and relinquishing a huge desire not to have anything to do with him ever again, we forged a synthesis of both wheels. It incorporated some beautiful psychological techniques, which we believed would provide a wonderful vehicle for change, and facilitate personal growth for participants.

Before our eyes, change occurred; not only among the participants but between ourselves. The energy between us changed. We were more relaxed in each others company; less argumentative, and more trusting of each other. Generally, we both seemed to be having a good time. And then we noticed it; that sparky energy you get when you are excited to see someone, or looking forward to their phone call. It sounds perfect, but at the time I was having none of it.

I'm not sure if he was driven by lust or wisdom, but I remember him saying to me that if we didn't experience the energy how would we know if there was really anything there? What ensued was a nonsensical, even farcical comedy, whereby he kept asking me to kiss him, and I would less than graciously decline.

I could make lots of excuses as to why I said 'no', but in reality I was afraid. I was afraid I might actually like it, and then what? I might have to let this man not only into my life, but God forbid, into my heart.

I'm not sure how long this farce continued, but I know what changed my mind. There were two things, actually. Firstly, the sparky energy didn't dissipate. It remained, whether we were together or apart. Secondly, I became aware of how much I was limiting my experience of life. I had so many rigid beliefs about how I should be; how I should act and behave. I was so locked in my own internal prison that I was unwilling to experience a kiss; a kiss, that sweet moment when two souls allow their bodies to touch and connect. I might like it, I might not, but how would I ever know if I didn't try? Did I run into his open arms full of wild abandon and passion? Hell, no! Instead, in a much more clinical and unromantic way, we puckered up, and I think after what seemed like the prerequisite one, two, three … we kissed. And I felt … absolutely nothing. I was so relieved. Later, he admitted that he felt like he had jumped out of his body, and witnessed the kiss without experiencing it.

Now I could breathe. Everything was okay. We could get on with our lives, and teach our Medicine wheel. After being lulled into a false sense of security we realised that the sparky energy didn't go away. So we decided to kiss again. This time it was delicious. It was like sweet nectar from the Gods, where our individuality melted away. We simply and sweetly became one.

I must add at this point that for me, after kissing and making love to one person for a very long time, it took a while to figure out exactly how we fitted together. Both of us were used to interacting in our own unique way, so there followed an adjustment period where we endeavoured to carve out our own particular style.

Holding hands, hugging, snuggling, and making love were now unfamiliar territory. How did you do it with someone new?

Initially, I hated the awkwardness. I was feeling raw and vulnerable, and I found the jarring nature of our togetherness daunting and unsettling. Eventually, in an attempt to get past this juncture I decided to look on the whole scenario as an interesting adventure. This was an opportunity to experience something new, with someone new. So we kept practicing and letting go of how we used to do things with someone else. I am very happy to report that we have been fitting together beautifully ever since.

The start of any new relationship is a magical time. You revere each other as God and Goddess; lovingly infatuated by every aspect of your new found mate. You relish each moment of this honeymoon period, and languish in the perfection of your new found coupledom. I savoured the excitement of our time together, which somehow seemed to shelter me from my internal turmoil. Over time, however, my inner and outer worlds collided. I couldn't hide myself in my new world, and I couldn't hide my new world from myself. As I struggled to come to terms with loving myself, I had to honestly and frankly ask myself, "Am I capable of loving this man? Have I the capacity to love, if I am only learning to love myself?"

The more I analysed myself the more I realised that a rather large part of me didn't believe that I could do it. I told myself that I was too selfish to love. On and on the self flagellation went, until I wore myself out listening to myself. Strange as it may seem, my saving grace came in the form of my two beautiful dogs.

One day, in a blinding flash of clarity, I realised how much I loved them. I loved them completely and unconditionally. And more importantly, they loved me. Here in my life was a channel of love so pure, and yet I had overlooked it in my despair. If I was capable of love in one aspect of my life, then I was surely capable of it in other areas. That is when I realised the power of the ego mind. The 'Divine Me' knew that I was loving, and lovable, but the job of the ego is to separate you from the Divine. It longs to keep you dwelling in the shadows, and in this instance it had done a remarkable job.

Relieved and excited, I re-embraced the relationship, but I had under estimated the insidious nature of the ego mind. Almost immediately, a new set of demons were unleashed. "You may be capable of love", whispered the ego, "But should you really love him? He has too much baggage and too many other priorities. He's too old. He's not trustworthy. And you know that he is going to break your already fragile heart."

On and on it went. Some days I could remain detached like a spectator, and watch as it taunted me with its jibes.

Some days when I was tired and delicate it lured me into its web of deceit. As I drifted in and out of meltdown, exposing all aspects of my vulnerability, he was patient and understanding. He shared his wisdom, compassion and experience with me to help me navigate through this difficult time.

My other saving grace was my awareness. When we were together, and connected with each other (heart to heart), everything felt easy and effortless, and all the incessant doubt-filled mutterings began to fade away, and were replaced instead by love. I recently read a lovely quote by Sobonfu Some. She is author of '*The Spirit of Intimacy*'. In it she says that, regarding life experiences, you can either "Go through them, or grow through them." I have a heartfelt belief that this relationship has provided me with a beautiful opportunity to grow. As a result of this relationship I have opened my pipe to love, and allowed it to help me let go of old limiting beliefs. It has also shown me that it is okay to let someone see you in all your vulnerability and rawness, and, miracle of miracles, they tend to love you more, not less.

Why then did I become so incensed with rage when I rang this lovely man and asked him for advice? Hell, I didn't understand. What I did know was that this energy was familiar. I had felt it before. It had happened a few times in the past, most notably when taking a work-shop on the teachings of Peruvian mystic Don Americo

Yabar. Don America's work is based upon opening yourself up to the Divine energy of creation, or to use its common name, Love. It seemed that everyone else at the workshop was blissed-out with the love vibration that was generated from doing the energetic steps. I, on the other hand, got angrier and more frustrated as the day progressed. Frequently, when I used these energetic steps afterwards a similar feeling arose. Confused and annoyed, I employed a self hypnosis technique, and was startled with what began to unfold.

It didn't come as a surprise to me that I was an expert in control. It had been part of my safety mechanism for a very long time. What did come as a surprise to me was how, as a result of control, I limited my ability to love. A year after separating, I saw my ex-husband, and was taken aback by how much love I felt for him. What transpired during the self hypnosis was that the reason I felt so much love for him was that it was safe to love. It was safe because we were not together. Both he and I were in new relationships, so there was no need to control the flow in the pipe. There was no chance that, in loving him now, I could get hurt in any way. He was no longer part of my life. I was no longer part of his. As a result there was a safety attached.

When I had spoken to my partner about my conundrum with this chapter, he pointed out mistakes and inconsistencies. Instead of being delighted with his help, I felt that all my buttons had been pushed. I wanted to slam down the phone and rip him apart. The reason I was so annoyed at him (and I know this sounds like the rantings of a mad woman) was because, the more he spoke, and the more enthusiastic he became in helping me, the more I realized he loved me. He saw beyond what I deemed to be my literary imperfections, and loved me anyway. What I have come to realize was a pattern that I constantly repeated with him. I continually looked for reasons to be annoyed and pissed off with him so that I didn't have to open my pipe to him. From a place of genuine love and support he consistently challenged my desire to avoid surrendering control of the flow of love between us. In doing so I had to let him in.

The reason Don Americo's energetic steps aggravated me so much was because they ask you to let go of control. They ask you to step uncontrollably into the energy of love. The ego, however, is very smart. It knows how to entice you. I had unwittingly been colluding with it for a very long time. The ego used anger as its henchman to distract me from losing control. If I was busy being angry I couldn't surrender to love. Then, in an ironic twist, the ego took control of me. Once I chose, even subconsciously, to wallow in the anger, I dealt a winning hand to the ego, and allowed it to separate me from the Divine.

This is why, although the exercises in the previous

chapter are incredibly helpful, they are not complete. Even though we are sending and receiving both love and forgiveness, we are still, in many respects, controlling the pipe. To understand, and to genuinely embrace the energy of love, we must in fact, go beyond.

When a tiny seed is nestled in the warmth of the earth, it doesn't decide that that's its lot. It doesn't remain content to stay that way for the rest of its life. Instead, it chooses to go beyond. It cracks open its outer husk, and reaches its delicate tendrils out into the world. After feeling the air above it, and the earth below it, through its newly developed shoots, the seed does not stagnate and wallow in its magnificence for succeeding at this momentous task. Again, it decides to go beyond. The tendrils connected to the earth reach even further down, sending roots into the fertile soil. The tendril that is caressed by the wind reaches up, and expands to become a stem.

And still, it goes beyond. The roots reach deeper into the soil, as the stem grows leaves, and unfurls them graciously to the world at large. And still it goes beyond. The roots suck moisture and nutrients from the earth to feed its sky borne limb, and still it goes beyond. A bud appears, perfect and intricate, and still it goes beyond. The bud uncurls to unveil its precious flower, never yielding to stagnation, and still it goes beyond. The petals wishing to experience flight detach from their womb-like nest, and choose to go beyond. New seeds are now revealed, gripping tightly around the stamen, and yet they go beyond. They launch into the breeze, and once more they go beyond. Some tiny seeds will come to rest once again in the warmth of the earth, and in time they will choose to go beyond. Some will become mulch and feed their sisters, for they have chosen to go beyond.

As we progress in life we become reluctant to choose to go beyond. We curtail our once childlike wonderment, and instead we invite stagnation into our lives. We tell ourselves that if we maintain the status quo everything will be alright. We do this in many, many ways. For some of us it means we never say what we are feeling, so that we can avoid an unsettling argument. In reality however, the emotion gets pushed down deep inside, becoming toxic and corroding our souls. For some of us we choose not to change jobs, partners, or neighbourhoods, telling ourselves that, all things considered, it could be worse. Yes it could, but you know, it could also be a whole lot better.

We take the same route to work, have the same breakfast, and hang out with the same friends, congratulating ourselves on feeling so content. 'Content', with all due respect to the English language, is such a nothing word, and yet we commend ourselves for taking up abode in the vacuousness of contentment. Contentment means that you are neither happy, sad, elated, nor depressed. You may say that you would rather be content than depressed, but at least you are feeling something when you are depressed. Contentment is a mind and body numbness that we use to validate our unwillingness to go beyond.

I remember at an early point in our relationship (when I was actively enjoying the kissing!), saying to my partner that he ticked all my boxes. What I meant by that was that in my head I had certain notions of what I would like my lover/partner to be; tall, handsome, smart, funny, loving, experienced ... blah blah blah. As time went on, I convinced myself that, because he ticked so many of my boxes, he must of course be my perfect mate.

For anyone who has ever been in a relationship, they know that, as time goes by, what they really get to see are the aspects of their partner that they failed to notice during that first flush of excitement when they were getting to know each other. You also begin to relax in each others company. High heels get replaced with trainers, and you start to lounge in your comfy clothes, instead of spending hours pouring over what to wear.

As our relationship progressed, I realized that, while he did in fact have many qualities that ticked my boxes, he also had a suitcase-full that did not. I struggled with convincing myself that it had been a beautiful love story, but it was not meant to be. It was something that the universe had put in my path to help me move on. And wait for it, my personal favourite, we were two souls who had travelled through life times to meet each other, and now our journey together was done.

In case you haven't already guessed, it gets very busy in my head. Thankfully, my awareness was blessed with more sense than I. For every reason that I came up with that validated why I should leave, my awareness continued to steer a different course. In the midst of my self-generated hysteria it would settle and reassure me that everything was going to be okay. It would allow me to pause long enough to take a breath, and listen to my own, and sometimes my partner's, advice to stop. It would allow me to connect with something greater than myself, which for me was the Divine.

I would visualise being held in the arms of angels. In moments, and as if by magic, the hysteria would disappear. I would gaze into the eyes of this handsome man and wonder what in the name of God had all the fuss been about. What I have come to understand is that someone is your perfect mate, not because of the boxes that they tick, but because of the ones that they don't. Having someone tick your boxes is a bit like having a love affair with yourself. You are willing to love them because they have qualities that you are comfortable with. Simply put, you love them because you have control.

We dress it up and say, "Oh, they are the person that I always dreamed of." In fact, what we really mean is, "There are certain qualities that I would like a mate, or a friend, to have, which won't challenge me beyond my emotional comfort zone. As a result I know that there will be very little chance of getting hurt. Because I now feel safe I will allow myself to love them and accept some love in return." In other words, "I will, at all costs, control the pipe." When we look for a partner that will tick our boxes, we automatically limit the adventure, and the love that we are willing to experience with them.

The other ego trap that I personally allow myself to fall into, which limits my love experience, is jealousy. I used to have a great theory on jealousy. It went something like this. It's alright to be jealous. In fact, I'm sure that I read that jealousy brings your attention to something that you would like to have in your life; the ring, the job, or the mate. Jealousy is a feminine trait. It helps bring out your passion, and once you don't hurt anyone with it, it's really fine. Yes indeed, the ego and I were well and truly in cahoots with each other.

What I have learned from my own personal experience is a lot less fanciful. Jealousy, quite simply and instantaneously, limits your pipe. When you are jealous, you believe that there is lack. You could be jealous that someone got a promotion, a new boyfriend, a new car, or that they became the centre of attention. You can be jealous that your mate loved someone else in the past, long before you were in their lives. The list goes on. Deep down, what you really believe is that the universe is not an abundant place; that everything is limited. If someone else is in receipt of the abundance, you believe that there isn't any for you.

There may indeed only be one promotion but there are always other opportunities, other relationships, and absolutely there are always other cars. The way jealousy separates you is two fold. It separates you from the person who actually received the abundance, because you allow yourself to feel hurt that they got something that you didn't. It separates you from God, because you think that God, for whatever reason, will provide for everyone else but not for you. Jealousy is a gut wrenching, heart twisting feeling that alerts you to the fact that you are allowing your ego, and some old belief system, to limit the flow in your pipe.

The lovely man in my life has two children that he loves dearly, and rightly so. Frequently, if I got a text or a phone call that he was going to pick up his girls or spend time with them, I would get that stomach churning feeling. I found it strange, as they are lovely kids. I now understand that what I was feeling was jealousy. If he was giving his time, and his love, to them, there was less for me. My ego self didn't like not being first on the pecking order, and I would automatically close my pipe, not only to him, but to his children as well. If I wasn't in receipt of a full love hit from him, I'd be damned if he or his kids were getting one from me. Yet again, the ego wins.

I know I have lingered on my own experience with regard to love. I do so because, instead of presenting you with a philosophical argument on how we limit our experience to love, I want to show you how, in practical terms we do it in everyday life. Look around you. Where have you limited the flow of love through your pipe to others today? Did it make you feel better, or did it make you feel worse? When we limit our capacity to love, we usually suffer too. In limiting ourselves, we separate ourselves from others, and from our vital life-force energy.

When it comes to love, we have many ways of limiting our experience. We talk about the love of a parent for a child, the love we have for our friends, our families, and our pets. We talk about romantic love, and unconditional love. Basically what we are doing is categorizing love, and limiting our experience of it. Even in talking about unconditional love, we are loving on the condition that we let go of conditions. This is a belief system that, in turn, generates a limited experience.

I appreciate that for some people the very concept of love is a difficult one to come to terms with. For me, love is a complete body sense. It feels like a warm glowing sun, radiating in my chest. It brings a smile to my face.

I feel warm and tingly inside, while at the same time feeling completely at peace. My body relaxes as I become present in the moment. All thoughts and concerns about what has passed, or what has yet to happen, disappear, and I feel completely connected to the Universe.

All sense of limitations and isolation disappear. Sometimes the feeling is mild; a gentle flutter. Sometimes the feeling is incredibly intense, so much so that I feel like my physical form has dissolved into love, and that nothing of me remains. Yet ironically I feel whole. For me, when I am 'in love' with myself, my partner, a puppy, or the Divine, I feel like my inner palette is radiating its full luminosity to the world, and causing the cells in my body to tingle in joyous response.

Do not confuse romantic love with Love. Romantic love is a conditional state. We are loving conditionally, based on our expectations of the relationship, or of our partner. It is as a result of this conditional state that we are able to fall 'out of love'. Love, in its essence, is an innocence that takes you back to the Divinity of who you are, so that you can see the Divine in another person, or in a moment. Love melts away the barriers we place between ourselves and our experience of life, and it centres us in the oneness of who we are.

Think of a time when you truly felt love, no matter how brief the moment. Allow yourself to take a couple of deep gentle breaths, and let an image of when you experienced a body sense of love to drift up into your consciousness. How does that feel? I'm guessing it felt pretty good, even if it was love from a place of control, with a limited pipe.

The wonderful news is that when we go beyond, we not only open the pipe, we actually expand the pipe, and allow even more of that gorgeous love feeling to flow through. How do we go beyond? We let our awareness show us when we fall into the trap of the ego. Then, when you are infuriated, annoyed, angry, upset, disappointed, and jealous, you love anyway. You open the pipe instead of restricting the flow. Closing the pipe won't make you feel better, and it won't take the pain away. But opening the pipe does.

I have honestly had to ask myself that if I had opened my pipe to my husband, could I have saved my marriage, and the answer is probably 'yes'. Time however has past, and I cannot turn back the clock, but I can use what I have learned to stop myself from repeating the same limiting patterns of behaviour in this relationship. What I am asking of you, and of myself today, is to go beyond. Go beyond the limits we place on ourselves when it comes to love.

I recently listened to Sonia Choquette, a well respected, vivacious psychic, and teacher, talk about living life to the edge. She was talking about not limiting your experience of life. By living life to the edge, you opened yourself up to a much more expansive and joyous adventure. In doing so, you also became a role model for others, and a catalyst for change. I love the idea of living life to the edge, but I think we should do that, and then you guessed it … go beyond.

Scientists who have been exploring space have discovered that, every time they reach what they consider to be the edge, there is more. What they have discovered is that when they bring their awareness to the edges of the known, the universe actually expands, so that they can go beyond!

You may ask yourself why is all this important, and why have I spent so much time, and so many words, trying to convey what I have learnt about love to you. The reason it is important is very simple. Unfortunately, the energies that prevail in our everyday world are fear, loathing, hate, control, frustration, and lack, to name but a few. How often do you dwell on the people or the events that annoyed or upset you during the course of the day? How many times do you finish the day by thinking about all the times, during that day, when you were touched by love? I'm guessing there is a deficit between the two for most people.

Look at the TV and the newspapers. Whatever your political position, you have to admit that, be it in the name of peace, God, or progress, we are committing atrocities against our fellow man and woman on a global scale. We are raping and pillaging the natural resources of the earth at a terrifying rate. This is not the energy of love. It is the energy of war. I know that this is quite a leap of faith for some of you, but all the indigenous spiritual traditions, no matter how diverse, agree on at least one thing; whatever is happening in your outer reality is a reflection of what is happening in your internal world. "As within, so without."

If we can change our internal world (i.e. ourselves) we can actually change the world. How completely mind blowing is that? If you come to a place of peace and harmony within yourself, it will cause a ripple effect out into the world at large. Like I said, this might be quite a leap of faith for some of you, but think about it. Think about a time when you were in a really good mood. Didn't that positive energy radiate out to everyone around you? If, on your path to womanhood, you could embrace self love, you could in fact by doing so, send a love vibration out into the universe that might change the world. By healing yourself, and by loving yourself, the world heals, and we tip the scales in favour of the positive instead of the negative. What a beautiful gift to bequeath to your friends, your families, your children, and yourself.

We spend so much of our lives hiding. We hide behind our woundings and our perceived failings. Daily, we present the masks we choose to wear to the world, in an attempt to avoid being seen or judged for who we truly are. Honour who you truly are. Open your pipe, and let the energy carry you beyond. You have no idea how big the pipe will get. It might even disappear, so that the confining limits of the pipe itself go beyond. In doing so, you will transform your life, and you also open yourself up to the possibility of transforming the world.

Stand naked in the world, proclaiming this is who I am; perfection in my imperfection; Divine loving creative energy made manifest. We all know the concept of loving unconditionally, but what I am asking of us is to love uncontrollably. When we love uncontrollably, we open ourselves up to the vastness of the universe. It doesn't mean that you have to hug everyone you meet in the street (you can if you want to) but it does mean that you bring your awareness to your pipe, and every time you notice yourself limiting the flow, you love uncontrollably once again.

When you start to do this it will at first be like a muscle that you have long forgotten to exercise. There will be aches and pains. Persist with it, and begin to watch out for the miracles that occur in your life. See how your relationships with people change. See how your relationship with yourself changes. Prepare yourself to bask in the daily outpourings of love that you receive from others, because if you are uncontrollably loving, there is going to be a whole lot of love pouring right back at you. Be a role model for your kids, your friends, and your community. When tensions run high and emotions are fraught, instead of battling with someone ego to ego, love uncontrollably, and allow that Divine energy to flow through you and provide you with new insight and wisdom as to how you may resolve the situation.

I am a reformed Catholic. Like many teenagers I rebelled against the church during my adolescence, and then during my feminist phase it became a convenient scapegoat to blame for all the wrong doings that had been done to women, and to society. However, I always loved the ceremony of church. I easily embraced the ritual and ceremony of other traditions, so at a point in my twenties I revisited my relationship with the church. I left aside all that I had found wrong with it. Instead, I looked beyond my own bias, and approached it with an open heart.

While there are still many things that I don't agree with, or approve of, regarding the Church, for me there is, at its core, a beauty to the ceremony which allows me to connect with something greater than myself. The reason I tell you this is because there is a beautiful little church perched on a hill beside the idyllic hermitage in which I am currently staying, and last night I felt the urge to go to Mass. The scripture was one that I have heard many times before. "Blessed are the peacemakers for theirs is the kingdom of heaven."

As I reflected on it afterwards a whole new meaning of those familiar words revealed itself to me, and I share it with you now. By allowing the radiant light of heaven to flow through us we become a channel for peace in our world, and not only is that a blessing, but we can also create a kingdom of heaven here on earth. Heaven doesn't have to be some outer reality that exists beyond the stars. It can be something that exists within us, and is reflected in the world around us.

Love is the transformative energy of the universe. Are you brave enough; courageous enough to love? Are you willing to love uncontrollably? If you are, you will change your life forever, and in doing so there is more than a slight chance that you just might save the world.

Exercise – Connecting to Love

1. When in your life have you experienced the feeling of love?

   It could have been triggered by a partner, parent, child, animal, friend, colleague, stranger, a movie, a sunset, a connection to the Divine, or a piece of music, etc.

   How long did the feeling last?

   What did if feel like in your body?

2. If love was a colour, what colour would it be?
   If love was a smell, what smell would it be?
   If love was a piece of music, what music would it be?
   If love was a taste, what taste would it be?
   If love was a touch, what kind of touch would it be?
   If love could speak to you, what would it say?
   Love is a feeling, not a thought. Now that you have awakened your senses to love take a few moments to rest in what it feels like, allowing the love energy to permeate through your body.

3. This exercise is based on Atisha's Heart Meditation:
   In this exercise you will use the heart, which is the energetic love centre in your body, to transform any heavy or stagnant energy that is present in your life. To do this you will breathe hate, fear, etc. into your heart, and breathe out love and compassion. I know that many of you will not savour the idea of breathing hate into your body, but remember nothing else can exist in the presence of love. So imagine your heart like a combustion chamber, where the heavy energy that you breathe in is combusted, and where the pure energy of love is released. This exercise is alchemy, because you take a heavy, dense energy and turn it into energetic gold; i.e. love.

   Keep focusing on your breath, and remember when the ego tries to taunt you into thinking that you can't do anymore, or that the exercise is futile, allow yourself to go beyond. Also let go of outcome. You are doing this exercise unconditionally, so you cannot do it in the hope that your mother will talk to you again, or that a war will cease overnight. That indeed may happen, but it is not for you to decide where the love vibration will weave its magic. Open your pipe to love, and trust the Universe to do the rest. Be open to the experience, and witness what happens in your body when you allow yourself to love uncontrollably.

- Close your eyes and allow your awareness to guide you to the areas in your life where you are limiting your pipe.
- Think about the people that you have an issue with or the situations that you are not feeling very loving towards.
- Pick the first person that comes to your mind and visualize your pipe extending from your heart out to the heart of the person you are out of balance with.
- Breathe the hurt, pain, etc. that exists between the both of you, into your heart. Allow the energy to be combusted, and breathe out love and compassion.
- Keep visualizing the person you are connected to, and continue breathing the energy into, and out from, your heart, until you feel the energy change between you.

The depth of the fracture between you and the person that you are working with will determine the amount of time you need to spend on opening your pipe. For some people this will be done in one sitting, and for others it may be necessary to repeat the meditation for several days or weeks before the heavy energy completely abates and is replaced by love.

Repeat this exercise daily for at least a month, working with the people, or situations, with whom you have issues. It could be yourself, your mother, daughter, sister, husband, boss or a co-worker, etc. All the time, breathe in the hate, fear, resentment, anger, and jealousy, allowing it to be combusted, and allow love and compassion to flow back down your pipe.

When you have finished breathing in the dense energy between you and the people in your life, extend your pipe out to the world. Extend it to countries where there is war or famine, or to politicians, or world leaders that you don't like. Breathe in the hate and hurt, breathe out love and compassion.

When you are finished, take a few centering breaths. Allow your awareness to come back to your surroundings, and gently open your eyes. You may wish to make some notes in your journal.

The more you do this exercise, the more you increase your capacity to love. In time your pipe will expand, and you may even go beyond the limits of the pipe itself.

This is a beautiful exercise, and deceptively powerful in its simplicity, but it does take courage, and a willingness to let go of your desire to maintain control, and to hold onto the hurts that exist in your life.

The Fifth Stepping Stone
～ Death ～

"*If we honour the self, and can step into love, we must then be willing to die; not physically die, but we must be willing to let die all the parts of ourselves that no longer serve us, the 'old me'. This is a difficult request to ask of many people. They like the old version of themselves, and they are not willing to relinquish it in order to move forward. The ancient traditions remind us that there is no death. There is only a transition from one form of self to another. Death is merely a crossing. We must cross a bridge to get to new land, and so too must we cross from the old 'us' to the new 'us' if we are to return to the place of wholeness within ourselves. The old you served you well. It was your protection, your teacher, and your vehicle for change. But like the caterpillar morphing into*

197

the butterfly something has to be surrendered for something new to be born."

Death, you may be surprised to hear, provides a wonderful opportunity for life. Think about nature for a moment. As winter rolls in, and the days get shorter, and the nights get longer, we enter into the death period of our calendar. The foliage on plants and trees die away. Their leaves return to the soil, to mulch. The winter winds and rain strip away old branches and foliage, and naturally prune back the landscape. And the earth, she sleeps. After months of nurturing new growth and new crops, and guarding her offspring until the autumn harvest, Mother Earth rests. She rejuvenates herself in the dark cold days of winter, until the new light and warmth of spring awakens her from her slumber, ready to start again. We have much to learn from the Earth. If we allow all that is old and rotten to die away, we can enter into our inner darkness, where we can rest, reflect, restore, and emerge renewed.

I am a bedfellow of death. I have called to her often over the years when times were tough, and all I wanted to do was sleep the great sleep. Some traditions will tell you that this is pointless. They say that your soul has contracted to learn certain lessons during its lifetime, and if you cut this life experience short, and forfeit the opportunity to learn, you will bear the karma, and have to retake these lessons, as well as a few more in the next lifetime.

Personally, when I was tired to the bone, and emotionally exhausted, that was a chance I was willing to take. Death to self, however, is not about sleeping the great sleep. Instead of opting out of life, it is in fact opting to live. Death to self takes courage, and is a huge uncontrollable act of self love. If you allow yourself to die to yourself, you suddenly become available for life. Any aspect of our lives that we cling to, which are old patterns based on our woundings, or old beliefs or behaviours which we have outgrown, generate stagnation in our very being. The more stagnant we are the less we are available for life, as the heaviness of stagnation strangles our vital life force energy. We must love ourselves enough to let the old parts of ourselves die away so that the 'new you' can be born. This allows you to love yourself even more. It is a beautiful cycle of discovery and self growth, where you come to a deep knowing of who you truly are, if you are willing to embark on the journey.

The journey of the feminine is an inner journey. Carolyn Hillyer, in her book *The Oracle of Nights*, describes this as a journey into the Cave. "It is a personal territory of darkness and shadow. It is an intimate underworld." As women, we must journey into the underworld of our being so that we can relinquish the aspects of our lives that are outmoded, as well as the relationships that have run their course, and the belief systems that have ceased to serve us.

The first time I encountered the transformative power of death was when I was a student of the Medicine Wheel. On working with each healing modality, or direction of the wheel, you encounter a body of wisdom that takes you through your healing process. The West direction of the wheel is represented by the energy of Jaguar. She is the huntress, the tracker, and the bringer of death. Jaguar helps you track to the core of your being to find the areas of stagnation that no longer serve you. She invites you to let them die so that you can grow and flourish. You face your shadow so that death no longer stalks you. This sounds like an interesting adventure. The stark reality was not nearly so pleasant.

I have doubted many things in my life, but my one saving grace was always God. Like any relationship I sometimes felt annoyed, infuriated or separated from God, but I never doubted the presence of a higher power. I clearly remember the last day of our West direction. I was sitting in class, and out of nowhere I was hit by the thought that this was all a load of nonsense. God, shamanism, and everything that went with it, was something fantastical that I had bought into, in order to make myself feel better.

There was no other life, or other beings. There was only this life. You lived, you suffered, maybe you got to be happy, and then you died. The End! Everything else was an illusion that I had created, an imaginary world, so that I would have a sense of purpose. All these people in the room with me, in an attempt to make themselves feel better, had bought into the same illusion. Everything that I believed in started to disintegrate. There was no God. There were no spirits. I was talking to nothing, and fabricating a response. Maybe I was insane, or maybe I once was but now I was sane. How could I tell the difference?

It felt like everything that I had identified with, and felt close to, died away. I wasn't the person I thought I was. The world wasn't the place I thought it was, and all my interactions with myself, and the world, were based on a fantasy. And so it went on for weeks on end. Each day, death consumed another part of who I was, or something I believed in. A part of me tried to rationalise that I was experiencing the West energy of the Medicine Wheel, and another part of me was sure that the Wheel was part of my fantastical illusion.

I was ripped apart during the months that followed until eventually I was lost in the abyss of nothingness. Somehow, while lost in the nothingness, I managed to find myself. I cannot really explain how it happened. I became aware that everything I had believed in had actually been someone else's beliefs. My beliefs about God had come from my church. My beliefs about shamanism had come from my teachers and mentors. My beliefs about who and what I was had come from my family, my peers, and society, to name but a few. So little of what I believed in was my own truth.

I had been living my life, based on the beliefs and ideals of the significant people in my life. Even when I had rebelled in my late teens, I realised I had taken on another set of rebellious teenage beliefs. I had acquired the beliefs of feminism, and the anti-church movement. I had merely exchanged old dogmas that I had grown up with for new dogmas that I had discovered in college. Now as all the dogmas fell away, I had to discover what was true for me. What did I think about life, people, the world, myself?

Initially, this was not an easy process. What I realised was that I had to stop thinking for myself, and start feeling for myself. So many of my thoughts were other people's thoughts, but my feelings were my own. When I took my awareness away from my mind, and brought it down into my body, where I could connect with my feelings, I could discern how I felt about the world. I might be verbally voicing an opinion to the world, but if I checked in with my feelings, I knew instantly if I really believed in it or not. Instead of going along with everyone else's flow, I started to tune into my own. The more I connected with my own inner truth, the more confident and self assured I felt. The harrowing pain of the preceding months gave way to a more authentic expression of me.

If you have ever experienced death in your life, you will know that it is a heartbreakingly painful process. The loss of a loved one rips you to the core of your being. You are raw, juggling a plethora of emotions, including sadness, anger, guilt, shock, disbelief, gratitude, loss, and heartbreak, all of which can be vying for your attention at any given time. When you have been touched by death, it feels like someone has pressed 'stop' on the movie reel of your life. You no longer know what the future will bring, but you know that life can not possibly be the same as it was before. So why would I ask you to willingly invite death into your life?

Death is a painful experience, and yet for as long as I can remember I have always enjoyed the solemnity and ritual of it. I love the tradition of laying out the deceased at home. I love people coming to pay their last respects. I love that, in a room full of sadness and heartache, we can also share stories of the joy and laughter that we enjoyed with our loved one. I love the prayers and the ceremony of returning our beloved back into the loving arms of the Earth.

One thing that I always find fascinating about death is that you often realise that you never really knew this person that passed away. However, this person may have played a starring role in your life. Many times when I have been at wake or funerals I have heard stories about someone I thought I knew, only to find out that there were many aspects of them that I had not witnessed. When we die, all the people from the various staging areas of our lives come together, and over tea, sandwiches, or a 'wee drop of Irish', put the pieces together that make up the puzzle of our lives. You hear stories of kindness, wildness, old heartaches, and secret romances. You hear about forgotten friends, holidays, and adventures. You hear about depressions, illnesses, and money lost and gained. Quite often, by the time you have interred your loved one into the earth, you feel like you have only gotten to know them, and now they are gone. Why is this?

We go through life compartmentalising ourselves. We often present different personas to the people at work, to our kids, our partners, and our families. We tend to present the version of ourselves that we perceive will be liked, in any given situation. To be liked and loved is a basic human need. In looking for acceptance and love we adopt the role that we perceive will make us most likeable in each situation; the joker, the nurturer, the vamp, the leader, the follower, the sister, the daughter, the boss, the employee, and on and on the list goes. In each role that we assume, we share a part of ourselves but we never unveil the whole picture, in case we are not liked.

We do this mostly unconsciously, but often we are very aware of what we are doing, and we go to great lengths not to let our guard down. If we love ourselves unconditionally, and uncontrollably, we cease having to present different versions of ourselves to the world. We are centred in who we are, showing our essential essence to the world, both light and shadow; our own unique glorious nature, warts and all. This takes a lot less energy, for you are simply you. You cease having to maintain the multiple versions of your various identities, yet for many people this is a terrifying thought.

We resist being ourselves, in case we are not liked, and ultimately not loved. We believe that the more personas and roles we assume the more chances we have of winning love in the great love lottery of life. We take on other peoples and societies belief systems, so that we can fit in and belong. The truth is that, as we divide our essence into little pieces, and sing to someone else's tune, we become fractured both to ourselves and others. We lose our sense of self, and those around us never get to know us and love us in our entirety, because they only get to witness a fraction of who we truly are.

Being 'all things, to all people' leaves us exhausted, as well as lost and confused within ourselves. We tell ourselves that this is life and you just have to get on with it. That would be wonderful except that most of us are not getting on with our lives. We are stuck in a constant state of emotional inertia. We are not living lives bursting with passion and joy and fun and laughter and abundance. We are instead exhausted from what we call 'modern life'. We multi task and multi role, getting caught in the hum drum of life. We hope that if we can stick it out for long enough, and if we are lucky enough, something might change. We feel fractured, and yet long to know our purpose in life.

The intention of this book is to help you to move from the sluggishness of emotional inertia to the bustling vibrancy of life. Hopefully you will find yourself, your true self, in the process. The bridge we must cross, on our journey from inertia to that vibrant life, is death.

We have a natural fear of death. Our fight or flight mechanism is programmed to keep us alive, so why would we surrender to death? The irony is that death to self brings us closer to life, and allows us to leave the limitations of fear and suffering behind. Imagine for a moment that there is a radiant light that shines from within you. This light is your essence, your full potential. Like a lighthouse you beam out into the world, radiating your divinity for all to see. The brighter and stronger your light, the more dazzling and exquisite you are. You can light up peoples lives just by your very presence, and the people that are drawn to you emanate a similar radiance. Life is full and vibrant and joyous.

Imagine that every negative or limiting belief you

have about yourself dims your light. Every bit of stagnant energy that you hold onto from the past also dims your light. The negative emotions that you carry also minimises your radiance. If your lighthouse is full of junk and clutter it obscures the bulb, and prevents your light from shining in its full capacity.

When we die to self, we allow everything that limits our inner radiance, our true Self, to fall away. A bit like a tuning fork or a musical instrument, everyone can be compared to a note. When we resonate to our own unique note, the music we create, either on our own or in union with others, is sublime. If we block our resonance, our note becomes jarred and discordant. Agony and suffering are generated from clinging to thought forms, beliefs, or energies that do not resonate with our essential self. If we embrace death we allow ourselves to simply be our light, our essence, our note.

In order to embrace death, we must first bring our awareness to the process that we are entering into. Death in energetic terms is a crossing, a transition from one aspect of our lives to the next. In tribal cultures rites of passage very clearly mark pivotal transitions for members of the community. Birth, coming of age, courtship, marriage, and becoming an elder are marked by ceremony and ritual. When an individual goes through a rite of passage they willingly surrender their former identity. In bearing witness to the individual's transition to a new aspect of their lives, the members of the tribe are lending their support to the initiate's declaration that they are ready to surrender their old self and step completely into their new identity.

Few of you reading this book will be doing so from your tribal village, yet whether you are from a rural or urban environment, rites of passage are equally relevant. If we do not constantly relinquish the old, the lines between the past and present become blurred. This limits the ability of our light to shine as it becomes polluted with old personas and beliefs that we have outgrown.

Nowadays, women live longer, and as our life experiences become more varied than those of previous generations, the necessity to mark the different aspects of our lives becomes increasingly imperative. As we go through a continual process of metamorphosis we must leave the old identities behind. Child, teenager, adult, career woman, married woman, single woman, new parent, divorcee, parent of adult children who have left home, changing career woman, retiree, adventurer, widow, wise woman, and old woman are some of the stages that we may go through in our lifetime.

For most of us, one stage morphs into the next, and this is what we have come to recognise as normal. Take a moment to try and feel the difference it would bring to your life if each new stage you entered was witnessed by your peers, friends, or loved ones. How would it feel to honour the life you have led up to each pivotal point? Give thanks for it, and then consciously let it go, so that you can step forward into a deeper, richer expression of who you are.

Much as I wanted to get married there was a part of me that did not want to completely surrender my single persona. My inner feminist protested as to why I should have to take on my husband's surname. Why didn't he take mine? This was another example of men dominating women. What I came to realise was that by hanging onto my maiden name there was actually a part of me not willing to die to my single life. I was not willing to step fully into being a married woman. It was not that I wanted to play the field and keep my options open. What I was unwilling to do was surrender my complete independence, and step into an interdependent relationship with my husband.

Thirteen months later I said goodbye to the old me. I changed my name, stopped being a Miss, or a Ms, and finally became a Mrs. No one was more surprised than me that it felt really good. In letting go I was able to honour who I had been as a single woman. I was able to honour all that she had given me, and taught me, and all the fun and adventure that I had enjoyed. In consciously leaving behind my single self, I could embrace my married self. I could be open to the new adventure and experience that lay before me.

Similarly, on the morning when my husband and I finally separated, I left the house on my own. My husband had been there in the morning, as he was going to continue to live in our house. I heard the front door close, and I knew he had left. Some friends came to help me move my belongings but he stayed away. The pain for him, I found out later, was too great. There were no goodbyes, no last words; no "I'm sorry".

When we legally separated some months later, I signed a piece of paper in front of a solicitor, again on my own, which was to bring our marriage to an end. I remember saying to her "Is that it?" Nearly 16 years of relationship wiped away by a signature. I remember coming out of the solicitor's office. Everything felt incredibly surreal. It seemed as if life was going on as normal around me, and yet for me, realistically and now legally, life would never be the same again.

I felt like I needed to do something to mark this day, but I was on my own. I had naively gone to the solicitor's office without any support, not knowing what to expect, or how I would feel. I found myself in a shoe shop buying two pairs of shoes, to have something to prove that this day really did occur, and that it was not some figment of my imagination.

It came then as no huge surprise to me that, a year after my separation, part of me still felt married. I still used my married name, and even though I rarely saw my ex-husband, I felt no sense of finality regarding our marriage. A therapist suggested a completion ritual that I could do with my ex-husband to honour each other, and finally let the marriage go. He was not interested in the ritual, but he still had all the photos of our time together, and was willing to meet me to sort through them, and go for lunch.

While sorting through the photographs, amidst laughter and tears, we walked back through our life together. When we went to lunch we talked about our life as a couple, as well as our families and mutual friends. We talked about how we were doing; our separation, our new relationships, our fears, and our hopes. Hours passed, and as I talked to this man who had been a huge part of my life, I remembered why it was that I fell in love with him. I also realised why we could not be together.

When we parted and went our separate ways, I felt a little sad, but mostly I felt a huge sense of freedom within myself. I had journeyed with this lovely man but now it was over. In honouring our relationship I could honour all the love and growth that it had brought into my life, and accept that if I was to move forward it was now time to leave the past behind. In letting go of my marriage, and my husband, I stepped once again into being single. But I was a different single woman than I had been before. The single woman that drove home that day was more self assured, had more life experience, and was rooted firmly in the present, instead of dawdling in the energy of the past.

When I shed my married name, and re-embraced my family name, it was not a step backwards. Instead, it was a reconnection to a part of me that had become lost along the way. Some people would say that, if I got lost along the way, perhaps I should never have gotten married. I disagree. In dying to my single life, I learnt so many wonderful things about love, relationship, friendship, truth, losing yourself, and finding yourself. In dying to my marriage I learnt about courage, conviction, humility, receiving, and non-judgement, to name but a few. Each time we die to an aspect of ourselves we learn more about ourselves. Death continually brings us closer to the essence of who we are. If we can learn to embrace it, rather than resist it, in time, death will bring us home to ourselves.

As we journey through life one part of our journey tends to merge with the next. When this happens we have no clear sense of who we are, or who we are becoming. Our sense of self gets jumbled up, and we lack clarity. For those of us that are no longer part of a tribal culture, religious ceremonies can mark these transitions in some way. I believe however, that for a lot of people the significance of these ceremonies has been lost. They have become an excuse for a party or a get together, while the deeper meaning of these particular rites of passage have been long forgotten.

There is absolutely nothing wrong with having a party. What a fantastic way to celebrate. Ideally however, we would engage in the psychological, emotional, and perhaps physical preparation that is necessary to explicitly state to ourselves, and the universe, that we are changing, before celebrating with a party. We tend to launch ourselves into the party phase of the process without having surrendered any part of our old identity. Our subconscious works on a symbolic level. Verbally telling ourselves, or mentioning to friend or therapist, that we are changing, or that we are moving on, is usually not enough for this information to seep down into our subconscious. When we perform a ritual, the symbolism of the ritual engages our subconscious. It connects with our core and we become aware that something about us is changing.

Many people are fearful of the word ritual and its connotations. A ritual simply put is a ceremony, a formal procedure that marks an event. Rituals can be very simple, or incredibly elaborate. A baptism, a bar mitzvah, a wedding, or a funeral, are all rituals that many of us are familiar with. You can design your own rituals to include elements that resonate with you. The first step is awareness. What is it your intention for the ritual you wish to perform? Elements should include that which you wish to honour (an aspect of your life, a relationship, a pattern that has somehow served you etc.), the essence, gift, or teaching from this part of your life that you want to carry forward, and the part of you that you are ready to leave behind. Rituals can include a fire ceremony where something symbolising the old is given to the fire, and something new is presented to you. They can include stepping over something, to mark stepping into a new part of your life. They can include candles, incense, singing, or poetry; whatever for you is an appropriate way to mark an important transition in your life.

As my ex-husband didn't want to do a completion ritual, I consciously used our meeting as our completion. I talked to him beforehand about still feeling married, and I mentioned my intention for the lunch. While together we honoured our life as a couple. We honoured what each of us had gotten from the marriage. We shared about letting go, and moving forward. When we hugged each other before departing I was very conscious that this was the last time that we would do this. In hugging him I thanked him, and I let him go.

Death to self can be a painful process. It takes great courage to look at the aspects of your life that are no longer working, or stunting you, and let them go. Death to self is a courageous act of love. Do you love yourself enough to die and let go of the old to make space for something delicious and new, even if you don't know what that new aspect of your being is yet? Do you love yourself enough to let go of being your mother, your father, your teacher, your preacher, your peers, or your woundings? Are you willing to allow yourself to step into your inner darkness, so that you can journey towards your radiant light, to the place that you will in time come to know as home?

Exercise – Who am I?

Current Patterns	Conditioning	Choice	Hearts Desire
Diet			
Exercise			
Lifestyle			
Family			
Sexual			
Recreation			
Work			
Beliefs			
Spirituality			

- In your notebook make a similar grid. You may wish to use the same headings, or add some additional ones. For each heading, write down your current patterns. So for diet, list all the types of food, snacks and drinks you eat during the day, as well as any supplements you take.

- For each food that you have listed tick whether you eat it from conditioning or choice, and say why. So for example, if broccoli was on your list, do you eat it because your mother told you to eat your greens, or because you choose to eat it because you like it? Another example might be what do you eat or drink as a result of an advertising campaign?

- In the final column, list what you would eat and drink if you were living a life of no limits, from your hearts desire; not having things because they were good for you, or because you thought you 'should' have them. Every now and again my heart desires buckwheat pancakes for lunch, with lemon juice. My head believes that pancakes are for breakfast. My healthy self believes pure carbs in the middle of the day are an unhealthy indulgence. Yet when I follow my hearts desire, my body, for reasons I cannot explain, feels really good. When you are finished, take a look at all three columns, and see how your life might be different, in all sorts of ways, if you followed your hearts desire.

Exercise – Making Space

I will pre-empt this exercise by reminding you that death brings personal discomfort. This is an amazing exercise, and out of all the exercises in the book, if you were only to do one, this is the one that I would recommend. That said, if done correctly it will be somewhat challenging, and it should push you past your comfort zone. So if you are ready to welcome the healing properties of death into your life, and say 'Yes' to life, this is the exercise for you.

All the various items you have in your home, including clothes, books, silver ware, photographs, jewellery, etc. hold an energy. They can hold the energy of the person that gave the item to you. They can hold the energy of how you were feeling at the time you bought them. They hold the energy of the association that you have attached to them, for example, "This vase always reminds me of the time we …"

Items passed down through generations hold the energy of the people they have been in contact with. Unless you are using the item, in time its energy becomes stagnant. The more stuff you have, the more stagnation that you are not only surrounding yourself with, but living in. Some people even put their stagnation into storage. Storage companies make a fortune every year by facilitating you to stagnate. Our homes and work spaces are an outward reflection of our bodies and our minds, so take a look around you today and see what your environment is saying about you.

This exercise is not about de-cluttering. Energetically, it works much deeper than that. It is an internal clearing on a physical, emotional and mental level. To invite something new into your life, you have to make space for it. If your life and your home is full of stagnant energy, you can do all the workshops you like. You can say endless affirmations, make wish lists, and vision boards until they are coming out your ears, but until you actually clear out the old, and die to that part of your life, the Universe has a difficult time trying to provide you with your hearts desire. More often than not there is no room for it.

You may say "I have already manifested things I desired", and that is probably true. But I would bet that the rate of manifestation took much longer than necessary, or that you didn't get quite what you asked for, because the Universe had to squeeze it into your already cluttered surroundings.

So if you are ready to say 'Yes' to life, and open yourself up to limitless possibilities, this is the exercise for you.

- With your journal and a pen beside you, sit or lie comfortably, and take a few deeps breaths.
- With your intention, connect to your higher power

or Spirit, whatever is most comfortable for you.

- Breathe deep into your heart.
- Gently allow your awareness to come into your heart, and when you get there, take a look around. What does it look like, smell like, sound like?
- Notice that there is a door in your heart. This is the doorway to your essence, your essential self. When you are ready, walk through the doorway.
- When you are inside your essence, notice what it looks like; the colours and the smells. What are the qualities of your essence? It might be words, colours, shapes, or a sense, etc.
- In this chamber there is another door. This is the doorway to all the people and events that have shaped you, and made you who you are. All the precious moments in your life are contained behind this door.
- When you are ready, walk through this door and take a look around. Who is there, what do you see? What are the memories that you have forgotten, the places you used to visit?
- When you are ready, thank everyone in this chamber for visiting with you today, and know that you can return here again. Before you leave here, ask yourself what one positive word would represent this chamber? You may wish to write the word in your notebook.
- Gently step through the door back into the chamber

that contains your essence. Again, thank this chamber for meeting with you today, and see what word comes to you to represent all the energy contained within. You may also wish to make a note of this word.

- Stepping back through this doorway, come back into the energy of your heart.
- Take three deep breaths. Feel your awareness come back into your body. Gently rock your body, opening your eyes, and bringing your awareness back into the present moment.

With the words that you have written in your notebook, which are a reflection of your essence, set an intention for the energy you would like both you and your home to radiate with. For example, if I was doing this exercise today my intention would be, "I intend that my home and every aspect of my being radiates the energy of fun, magic, liveliness, abundance, and love."

Pick a room in your home, and see what items or belongings in that room reflect the energy of your intention. Do this for every single item in the room. Take whatever items that do not reflect your intention out of the room. You can then decide whether to gift them away, or if they can be recycled, or if they need to be thrown out. When you are done, physically clean the room. Light a candle in the room to represent the energy you wish to radiate through it. Repeat this process for every single room in your house, including closets that may be under the stairs etc.

N.B. DO NOT put the items you have removed into storage. By doing this, you are moving your stagnation somewhere else.

For many people this causes discomfort because we are sentimental about items. If you are particularly sentimental about an item, firstly ask yourself does it hold the energy you want in your home. Secondly, ask yourself how often you spend engaging with the item. Most of us have lots of stuff to remind us of an important moment or occasion, yet we rarely visit with it. As can be seen from the meditation at the start of the exercise all the important people and events in your life are held in your heart. You don't need lots of stuff to remind you of them.

Out of nearly 16 years with my ex-husband I now have, after doing this exercise, 8 photos. They are photos of me mostly on my own, or with my siblings. They reflect the essence of who I am. I have no photos of my ex-husband, not because it is too painful to keep them, but because it would be too easy to keep them, and allow them to keep me lingering in the energy of the past. The love that we shared is rooted deeply in my heart. There is no need for trinkets and mementos.

When my lovely partner and I decided to live together I moved into his house. Even though I thought that I didn't hoard, and was very good at travelling light, it was difficult to fit my stuff, and his stuff, into one home. We realised very quickly that it was not only our stuff that was causing the congestion but all the collective energy attached to it as well. We set our intention that everything in the house would be a reflection of our current essence; two people starting a new loving chapter in their lives, both privately and professionally.

It was amazing to see how differently we viewed our belongings when we worked through the house room by room with a very clear intention. I had my wedding dress hanging in the wardrobe. Here I was starting a new relationship and I had a very visual reminder of my old one. I even had underwear that my ex-husband had really liked. He had ornaments that had been wedding presents, and gifts from old girlfriends. Even his old marital bed was in the house.

Room by room we went through the house, and any-thing that was not our essence, not only as a couple but as individuals, was either given to charity, recycled, or thrown out. We filled bag after bag and box after box, with clothes, shoes, underwear, photos, furniture, crockery, jewellery, books, linen and photographs. Even files got sorted through, and we shredded mountains of old paperwork. When I was finished going through my clothes I was left with the jeans, top, and underwear that I was standing in, and two dresses. Everything else in my wardrobe belonged to the person I used to be. They did not belong to the person that I was now or that I was becoming.

We had a shamanic ceremonial fire to symbolically let go of the people we no longer were. Among the things given to the fire were my wedding and engagement rings, some photographs, and my medicine bundle that I had for the duration of my shamanic training. When we were finished we cleaned and cleansed the house, and it felt gorgeous. It ceased to be a house where two people were trying to fit together, and instead it had become a home with a strong pulsating heart. The freedom and space we felt within our bodies, and within our minds, as we released the baggage of the past, was really amazing. I remember saying to my partner, "I don't know where I am going this year, but I do know that wherever it is, I am travelling light." I didn't rush out to buy new clothes. Any new additions to my wardrobe were carefully chosen to reflect the essence of who I was, and similarly with my partner.

I know people believe that, if you let go of stuff, you will discover in a weeks or a months time that you really need it. This, I believe, is the old you trying to pull you back into the past. For each item you let go of, thank it for what it has brought into your life. Let it go gracefully, and allow yourself to die to that old aspect of your life.

In surrendering the old, we honour where we have

been, and give ourselves an opportunity to say goodbye to who we used to be, or to people or events that are no longer part of who we are. We have made space so that we can align ourselves to the essence of who we truly are, and embrace the new in whatever form that it may manifest in our lives.

The Sixth Stepping Stone
⟶ Life ⟶

"*L* *ife is for the living. It may seem a ridiculous thing to say, but so many of us who are alive, are in fact dead. Look around at your friends, your families, your co-workers; how many of them are truly alive? When you walk down the street look into peoples eyes and see if you can observe the spark of creation that supposedly dwells within. For many souls their spark has been extinguished. Life had gotten the better of them, and they are literally biding time until they can check out.*

All is not lost. Once you are still breathing, and some traditions would say even if you are not, your spark, your life force, can always be rekindled. So think and be honest with yourself; are you alive? Do you greet each day with wondrous

*excitement, waiting for the mysteries of the day to unfold? Or do
you drag yourself out of bed, forcing yourself to repeat the same
ole same ole routine as yesterday? Do you see every encounter with
someone as a chance to learn, to laugh, or to grow? Or do you see
it as people inconveniently getting in your way to wherever you have
to go? Do you look at your children and think they are angels
incarnate, or do you see them as noise makers and dirt creators?
How do you view life; is it a hardship, is it a chore, or is it a
miracle that you have the honour to participate in? Life is for the
living. Are you alive, or are you dead?"*

Ever since I can remember I have been a people
watcher. When I was younger I used to make up
stories about who I thought the passer-by's were,
their lives, who they were meeting, etc. I used to get
lost in a fantasy world of my own creation, based on
the real life characters that I watched. As I got older
and learned more about life, I started to notice myself
in other people. I could identify with their feelings
and their moods because I had felt them too. When
I opened up to my intuition and became a psychic
I started to see the person behind the person. The masks
that people wore in public started to disappear, and I
would see the soul that dwelled within. Instead of the
angry guy who drives everyone crazy with his temper
I might have seen the scared lonely child looking for
attention. Instead of the Diva dressed up to the nines

I might have seen a girl lacking in self confidence, looking to be accepted and admired.

Similarly, I assumed people 'saw' me. It used to really surprise me when people would say, "You're so confident, bubbly, etc.", when I sometimes felt lonely and vulnerable inside. I still watch people. They fascinate me. One thing that I notice a lot about people is how and when they allow their inner light to shine. You can tell when someone's spark is ignited. Their eyes sparkle. They glow from the inside out. They look happy, loving, inviting, and fun to be around. Their body posture is relaxed and open. Their energy is contagious. When somebody's spark is ignited, it allows you to ignite yours too. It is that certain 'je ne sais quoi' that we so admire in others.

Imagine that your spark, your life essence, is a light switch. There is an 'On' and an 'Off' setting, over which you and only you have complete control. When you come into this world your spark is automatically switched to the 'On' setting. When your mum holds you, or when you feel loved, your spark glows brighter. When you are tired or cranky your spark may dim, but ultimately your switch stays in the 'On' position. When we are small, although the intensity (the voltage, so to speak) of our spark may vary, it always remains 'On'. When we get a little older, and we start to get chastised by the adults in our world for being ourselves, or being naughty, we start to use our 'Off' switch. We turn our spark 'Off' so that we can conform, or become invisible.

If we are unseen, or become the same as everyone else, we can't get into trouble for our 'sparkiness'. We also turn our spark to the 'Off' setting if we have been hurt or ridiculed. As our spark is our essence we can feel vulnerable once it is exposed. Once we learn that the world is not always a friendly place we hide our spark from others. Sometimes we hide it from ourselves, so that we remain safe and protected, shielding ourselves from future hurts that may remind us of the past.

Somewhere in our psyche we believe that hitting the 'Off' switch spares us from many of life's woes. This is not the case. All it does is facilitate us in feeling disconnected, distant, unavailable, lonely, uncommitted, and unhappy; and speaking from personal experience, numb. What I have learned is that the more we allow our spark to glow, until it ultimately ignites into a wondrous flame radiating life and passion, the less we get hurt. This is because we become more rooted in the sureness of who we are, and indeed who we can become. If you are connected to your spark, no words of criticism or reproach can affect you. You realise that the words are someone else's opinion, and when they come into your airspace your spark vaporises them on impact.

I've had many profound experiences on my healing journey. While the memories of some of them have faded away as the healings integrate, the sweet nectar of some of my experiences remain with me. They remind me of my progression and growth, and the lessons learned along the way. Recently, while on a tantra workshop, I was surprised that an aspect of being molested presented itself for healing. I thought the subject was most definitely done and dusted at this stage of my life.

As I rode the wave of emotions that took me deep into my vulnerability, I arrived at a place within myself where I could see my spark. I could see my spark filled with the essence of who I was, and I could feel it radiate solidly throughout the core of my being. I could see that, no matter what happened to my physical self, nothing could touch my spark; my essence. I was responsible for my spark. Only I had the ability to extinguish it, or to allow it to shine.

While watching people, I have noticed that the switch for our spark is predominantly in the 'Off' position. Take a look at the people you pass when walking down the street, or sitting in a coffee shop. Do the people around you, both male and female, look like they are glowing with their inner radiance? Often, when we meet someone we like, or take a call from someone we care about, the switch goes 'On'. Depending on the nature of the engagement the switch may stay 'On' for a period of time afterwards. In most cases however it goes 'Off' again quite quickly, as we get caught up in what we consider the hum drum of everyday life.

Notice how, if we see someone walking down the street with a smile on their face and a twinkle in their eyes, we view this as strange behaviour. Often, we assume that only an illicit encounter would generate such a display. Many people believe that it is impossible to have your spark ignited all the time. This is not the case. Look at young children. Life is a force, and life force oozes from them. When they have it you can't miss it. It is a force that glows from within.

There are several reasons why we restrict the ability of our life force to shine. Our woundings diminish our willingness to allow our light to be seen. There is also apathy. A friend of mine told me about how some of her middle aged friends had taken their seats in God's waiting room. They had raised their kids, retired, and now they were just waiting until God called their number so that they could check out. Their minds and bodies were still healthy, but they had become disassociated from their life force. They were waiting out the days and years until death came to call. They had become apathetic towards life.

One of the other ways in which we restrict our life force is conformity. A letter was printed in the *Letters to the Editor* section of the *Irish Times*, entitled *Mná na hEireann* (*Women of Ireland*). The author (a man) posed a question, wondering if anyone could remember what the women of Ireland looked like before they all dyed their hair blonde, covered themselves in fake tan, and stuck on false nails. It is a generalisation, but we seem to have become more concerned with what we look like on the outside instead of who we are on the inside.

Humans as a species long to belong. From early in our development men and women have gathered together in tribes for safety and support. A tribe as a whole benefits from the contributions of all the individual members. This does not mean that everyone is in agreement. Instead, the diversity of opinions and ideas (which you can also think of as a giant mixing bowl containing the essence of all the participants) creates a rich soup, full to the brim of creative expression, which in turn nurtures and feeds all of the tribe. The tribe can then benefit from the gifts and strengths of each individual member.

Tribal costumes in the western world may look very different to those of our indigenous ancestors. Bearing the markings of a tribe, however, is very much part of our everyday life. Business suits, designer clothes, football jerseys, baseball caps, oversized jeans, etc. all make a statement as to which social group (tribe) we wish to be identified with. Our desire to belong is often so strong that we sacrifice our individuality, and instead opt for conformity. If we dress the same way, have the same opinions, hang out in the same places, then we can be part of our chosen group, and we no longer have to be alone in the world.

There is nothing wrong with being part of a tribe. It is a wonderful way to learn about relationships, develop our social skills, and learn from others. But some of us have lost our way. Instead of honouring our own individual essence, and using it to nurture the tribe, we often seem to look to our modern tribes for our essence, and for our identity. Stop for one moment, and feel how your life might be different if, instead of doing all the things that you think you should be doing so that you belong, you listened to your heart, and allowed it to guide you through life. For most people that is an incredibly scary thought.

When we conform to a tribe we allow it to steer us through life, because we often lack confidence in ourselves, and we are too afraid to take control of our destiny. Honestly answer this simple question. When you are among your tribe (it could be your gym buddies, your work buddies, your girlfriends, or your family), how much of your essence is truly visible to them? How much of your uniqueness do you share with them? Do you hold back so that you won't upset them, or be the odd one out?

One thing to be aware of is that when we no longer wish to conform we tend to rebel. Becoming a rebel, while it may help you break off some of the shackles with which you have bound yourself, is not an expression of your life force. All you are doing is rebelling, usually from a place of anger, against an archetype that has become entrenched in your psyche. Instead of conforming to the norm you conform to the archetype of the rebel.

When I was a teenager, because I didn't want to be the good girl, I did all the things that I felt were the opposite. I wore black clothes, and what I considered 'alternative' make up. I purposely drank pints of beer, so that I wouldn't be considered lady like. I wanted to be cool. I hung out with guys who had motorcycles, and I wore different earrings in each ear, so that I didn't conform.

Ironically, I looked and acted like lots of other teenagers who were also not conforming. In our non-conformity we all looked the same. However, the rebel that I had become wasn't me. It was just another incarnation of someone I wasn't. It took a long time to understand that, as long as I was trying to be someone or something else, I could never be myself. If we instead connect with our essence, it can lead us on a path to ourselves. Rebelling comes from a place of anger. Self-leadership comes from a place of love.

Contained within your essence is the blueprint for who you are in your fullest potential. Life will lead you on a path of exploration to new things, and to new adventures, but to go forward in life, full of life, you must first rekindle your flame. Connect with what was there before; your essence that existed before you gave up hope, gave into your woundings, and gave up on your dreams. If you go back to the beginning you can find yourself once more. By using that information like a catapult, it can propel you forward to your desired destiny. Once you open the door to your essence, you open the door to all the delicious secrets about the joyousness and passion that you have been hiding, even from yourself.

To connect with your essence you must follow your heart. Your mind only tangles you in a web of illusion and ego. Yes, you must court the mind so that it works with you, but do not let it be the conductor of your orchestra. Your heart is the conductor, and if you listen to it everyday it will create an incandescent symphony. Follow your heart, your dreams, and your magic, and all the rest will unfold.

If you consciously embrace the energy of your heart there is nothing that you cannot achieve. Follow your dreams and the opportunities to bring them to fruition will automatically present themselves. Listen to your 'heart song'. It will guide you home to the essence of who you are.

Up until now we have been clearing the terrain of your inner garden. We have scraped away the debris that has smothered your landscape. The time has come to see what is germinating in your soil. If your garden is to bloom this is where we must ignite the life force that will transform itself into your inner paradise. In the previous chapter I asked you to surrender to death; to let go of the aspects of yourself that no longer served you. If you have shed the old I now invite you to reacquaint yourself with your essence, so that you can revel in the delicious-ness of Life.

Your womb is the energetic centre of creation. It doesn't matter if your womb has been removed, or if your child bearing days are over. The energetic function of the womb, which is to create, always remains intact. You can, if you choose, birth yourself from this rich delicious space. Imagine your womb as an empty cavern. In the floor of this cavern you will find a little hollow. In this hollow, protected from the elements and from the world outside, is your spark.

If you wish, you can feed this spark with kindling, so that it turns into a bright flame. The kindling you must use is all the dreams you have for yourself, including the ones you gave up on; your dreams of being a dancer, a playwright, an artist, a healer, a singer, a preacher, a teacher, a mother, or a soul mate. Whatever your dreams are, allow them to fan the flames.

Add your unique gifts to the fire. Your gifts many include your kindness, compassion, loyalty, patience, directness, humour, vulnerability, generosity, your sense of fun, and your love. Add your woundings, your heartaches, and heartbreaks. Our woundings are an important aspect of who we are. The fire does not take away the woundings. But it does allow us to absorb the teachings and the life lessons that we have learned because of them, and transmute the pain. The lessons from our woundings form an intrinsic part of who we are.

Finally, we add in a little fairy dust; your magic, so to speak. Sprinkle in the colours, the flowers, the dance moves, the songs, or the fragrances that symbolise those delicious, secret parts of yourself that you keep hidden from the world. Breathe deep, and give your breath to the fire, to fan the flames. Keep feeding your dreams, your gifts, your woundings, and your magic to the fire. They can stoke the fire that now burns deep in your belly. You need to keep feeding the fire until the flames fill your cavern with heat and energy.

Allow this powerful wild energy to run up your spine, spread out through your body, and inform every cell of your being with the essence of who you are. Let that energy spread into your eyes, and cause them to radiate with life, while bringing a smile to your face. Don't stop it there. Let the energy reach out beyond your body, and pluck on the luminous chords of your destiny, so that you can align to the people and places that resonate with the essence of your life force.

Once you start to stoke those flames in your belly

amazing things start to happen. First of all you redirect your course in life, and start to come back into flow. When you are in flow you are working with the current of life instead of pushing against it. The next thing that starts to happen is that your passion for life will be renewed. There is an interesting inter-relationship between your life force and passion. One feeds the other. The more you engage with your life force the more passionate you become, and the more you follow your passion the greater your sense of your life force.

Sometimes, when we start to reconnect with our passion, we first encounter layers of anger and rage. When we suppress our passion, and restrict its flow, it often contorts into rage. We can be angry that we have given up on our dreams, or that we don't feel good enough that we deserve them. We can be angry about hurts that we have endured. The problem with anger is that we often project it onto others. In doing so it stops us from taking responsibility for ourselves.

The other thing about anger is it just doesn't feel good. If you are angry, get it out of your body in a way that does not hurt you or others. Anger is a strong force, and usually requires some physical action to release it. I have found even the most 'Zen' people to be angry. They are simply better at repressing it.

Exercise – Exploring Anger

- Find somewhere that you won't be disturbed, and have several large pillows beside you.
- Think about the things that make you angry.
- Begin to thump the pillows, and while doing so, verbally express your anger.
- You will find that after a while the specific incidences that make you angry disappear, and instead you may get carried along in a stream of the emotion.
- Go past the point where you feel you have nothing left to scream, punch or cry about (there is often more hiding inside), until eventually you reach a place of stillness within yourself.
- When you are done take some time to integrate and rest.
- Repeat this exercise as you need it, to release other layers of anger that may be lurking inside.

It's okay to be angry, but it's better to release it in a safe way. Then the healing can start. When we free ourselves from our backlog of anger we make way for passion to come into our lives. The reason we often confuse anger and passion is that they are both forceful energies. Passion, unlike anger, is pure unbridled energy in its rawest form. It is the energy of creation, and of your soul's purpose. It is expansive, and when you start to live your life from your passion, your life doesn't feel good. It feels 'great'. When you engage with your passion it guides you to your soul's purpose.

Some people, especially those who like control, are fearful of inviting passion into their life. They fear the rawness and wildness of the energy. Unbridled passion can be reckless. You do not want to tame it. That's like turning an eagle into a chicken. The secret to working with your passion is to temper it with love. Go into your heart. Ask yourself, what aspects of your passion do you want to share with others? If it is recklessness and wild abandon, this is not passion. Yet, it is what many of us fear we may find if we go into that passionate energy.

Passion runs deep. It is the very embers from which you were created. To go into your passion is to go into your intrinsic self, and engage with the elements that must fuel your fire. Take dancing, for example. When you dance from your heart, you honour your body. You don't push it further than it is capable of. When you dance with a partner you take them into your heart, and from there you engage in a wonderful union of movement.

Passion should feed you. If it drains you, or hurts others, you are playing out of your passion from a wounding that lurks deep inside. A talented painter who paints until death may be in the flow of his passion while painting. But, if in painting he is causing harm to himself or those he loves, he is painting from a place of inadequacy or ego. If you allow passion to flow through your heart centre it invigorates you and all those who surround you. If it is causing damage, you are not in your heart.

Exercise – Exploring Passion

How do you do this on a practical level?
- Think about something that you are passionate about, or an activity that you would like to engage in, to see if it 'juices you', so to speak.
- Get a sense of it. What would the sights, tastes, smells, or surrounding noises be like?
- What might you be wearing?
- Who, if anyone, might you be with?
- Do you need equipment, or is it something you can do on your own?
- When you have a really good sense of the energy surrounding your passion, take all that delicious energy, and breathe it into your heart.
- See how that makes you feel, and be open to letting your heart tell you how you can share that energy, at first with yourself, and then perhaps with others.
- Notice how the images, tastes, and surrounding noises might change.

Your heart may 'temper' the initial perception of your passion. It may give you one that is authentic to the radiant essence of who you are, and not the perception of what you think you should be.

Initially, I was afraid to connect to my passion. When I used to peak at it from afar, it felt too wild to me. I was afraid that it would be too forceful and overpowering for those around me, and that it would intimidate those whom I loved. When I learned to take my passion into my heart, all of that changed.

When I get a sense of my passion, I see a woman, nearly naked, with long hair of reds and browns and yellows dancing at night around a blazing bonfire. She is primal and strong, and her eyes pierce right through you. I am afraid of her, and yet I am intrigued by her. I long for the raw energy that she embodies. The scene smells musky and damp.

When I start to breathe the scene into my heart, firstly there is resistance. As I continue to breathe, the resistance dissipates, and I feel my heart opening up. The scene begins to change. Night becomes day, and the woman is not dancing alone. She is surrounded by the women and men of her tribe. She remains strong with those piercing eyes, but they have been tempered with the softness of compassion. The scene smells sweet and light and fragrant, and I know that I have come home. To honour her, and to honour this energy,

I put on some music, and I dance. I dance her, this nameless woman who is the energy of my passion, from my heart into my body, and I invite her to guide me through the day.

When you allow your life force and your passion to flow through your body, you look physically different. Your skin becomes clearer, and your eyes get brighter. You hold your head high, and walk energised through your day. You will find that your body starts to look for the food and drink that fuels your life force. And your old self will look for the food and drink that dulls it. For example, my life force likes spices and hot food. It likes to eat little and often. If, for whatever reason, I want to sabotage my life force, I eat what I call damp foods; ice cream, chocolate, and heavy meals. For me, this dampens the fire in my belly, and it separates me from my essence. Be watchful of the foods that you eat and drink and notice if they are working with you or against you.

When you engage with your life force your experience of life opens up. You stop expecting others to provide the life that you want, or feel that you deserve. Instead, you become a creative being who manifests their hearts desires for themselves. You become an inspiration for those around you. All of a sudden there are more hours in the day. There is more joy, more fun, more laughter, and more love.

I recently heard about a woman who at 92 won the competition in her local community hall for 'Best Halloween costume'. She had crocheted the complete witches outfit, including the hat, by herself. The organisers had to wait to present her with her prize, as she was on stage, line dancing during the prize giving. Now that's a woman in touch with her life force! Life is for the living. Embrace it, share it, and allow it to set you free.

Exercises:

1. Use this mantra at the start of the day, and then repeat it frequently throughout the course of the day. The times that it is most difficult to use are often the times when it is most important to say it. For example, if you are tired, cranky, or worried about something, use the mantra, and allow it to bring you back into flow. The more you do it the easier it will get, and the more natural it will become to you.

• Using your senses, get an impression of what your essence might be like. Is it an image, a sound, a fragrance, or a feeling? It may even be a combination of several. When you have a sense of your essence, allow it to flow from the earth up through your body, and out into the heavens. For example, if your essence was a song, feel the song rising from the Earth.

Feel the music flowing through your body and then out into the heavens. Please note that, over time and with practice, the way in which your essence presents itself may change.

- Now repeat these words.

> *'The Glorious Essence of my being radiates through me right now."*

- Repeat this mantra often. You will find that it rarely has the same effect twice, but that each time you use it you will feel more connected to the essence of who you are.

2. Remember to breathe. Our life force depends on our breath. Take conscious deep breaths at intervals throughout the day. The breath allows your life force to flow, and clears stagnation from your system.

3. Connect with your passion, and allow it to guide you through the day.

The Seventh Stepping Stone
∼ Nurturing ∼

"If you are alive you must nurture your soul. Feed it lovingly, and treat it kindly. Love your environment, and allow your environment to nurture you. Do things that juice you up, be it listening to music, dancing, walking in the garden, sowing seeds, potting plants, walking, ice skating, tangoing, visiting art galleries or museums. Nourish your soul at every available opportunity, and if possible share the experience with someone. It heightens the energy."

Return to your garden frequently and tend to the seeds that you have sown. If you do not nurture your garden, weeds may choke new growth, or seeds may perish for lack of watering and support. That is why I have carefully chosen the word 'tending' in relation to your garden. It is an ongoing process, and like a garden the more you tend to it, the more it blossoms and grows. How many times have you gone to a workshop, read a book, or been inspired by someone that you have listened to, and then despite your best intentions, you let all that newly found motivation fall by the wayside? If you wish for your Inner Garden to blossom so that you can reap its harvest, you must nurture it, and tend to it lovingly.

Nurturing is a natural progression at this part of the journey. You have by now hopefully let go of the past, and you are in the process of opening your heart a little further everyday. You are embracing the passion of life, and now, beautiful lady, you need to nurture all that you are in the process of creating. Most of us are familiar with the concept of nurturing, but at this juncture I would like to prompt you to think about it a little differently.

There are two kinds of nurturing which, if you engage in them, they will allow your garden to flourish. Peripheral soul nurturing helps you to recharge your batteries, and it gives you time out to realign yourself with your essence. Principle soul nurturing is the electrifying sensation that feeds you when you follow your joy in relation to your passion and purpose. They are both connected, and one fuels the other.

For me, peripheral soul nurturing includes walking in nature, horse riding, dancing, having a massage, working in my garden, or having fluffy cappuccinos with my girlfriends. All of these feed my soul, and allow me to connect with aspects of my essence, so that I have the vitality and enthusiasm for principal soul nurturing.

For me, principle soul nurturing is teaching workshops. It sends waves of ecstatic joy and electricity through my body, and it allows me to connect with something greater than myself. When I teach, I feel that I am held in the arms of the Divine, where everything melts away and I become one with the Universe. I am in flow. I am my purpose, and the passion that vibrates in my body continues to fuel me long after the workshop has passed.

The other wonderful gift that the essence of principle soul nurturing brings to your life is that once you have experienced the energy, you can call on it at anytime. If I am not teaching a workshop I can still take a few minutes to breathe into that familiar energy, and allow it to infuse me with its radiance. That instant connection transforms me emotionally and physically. I feel lighter, connected, on course, and I glow from within, looking younger, sexier, and more radiant.

Another way to connect to your principle soul essence is to talk about it. Tell someone about what you love doing. Share whatever it is that gives you joy with another, and allow your enthusiasm and radiance to ignite the joy that lives within them. I have a friend whose soul purpose is to look after children with special needs. When she talks about her work there is a constant smile on her face, and she glows. When I come away from her I feel like there is sunshine in my heart. I do not feel any calling to care for children as she does, but listening to her talking about what is obviously her purpose inspires me to follow mine. If there is nothing in your life that, when you talk about it makes you radiate from the inside out, you need to start some peripheral soul nurturing.

As we are all different, we all have different pleasures that constitute peripheral soul nurturing. It doesn't matter what gets your juices flowing. What matters is that you do it. Many of us procrastinate, waiting for the time, the money or the opportunity to 'indulge' in our peripheral soul nurturing. Meanwhile your life force is fading, and the luminance of your essence is diminishing.

We wait until we get sick or exhausted from stress to take time out to nurture ourselves. Nurturing then becomes damage control, and instead of using it as a delicious tool to nurture our spirit, and allow it to grow, we use it to get us back on the straight and narrow. We do this until we crash and burn the next time, and then we repeat the cycle all over again.

Peripheral soul nurturing should be an ongoing

process. Ideally, include at least one peripheral soul nurturing experience in each day. If you don't know what works for you, start experimenting. Take a class, spend some time in nature, visit a spa, have your lunch outside in the sunshine, go to the beach, sunbathe naked, play your guitar, or sunbathe naked while playing your guitar. Peripheral soul nurturing does not have to take up a lot of time. It could involve taking time out for a really nice cup of tea or coffee, instead of having it at your desk. It could be reading that magazine you bought instead of letting it gather dust on the coffee table. What about wearing some fresh flowers in your hair and allowing their fragrance to infuse your fragrance?

Watch a movie that you have been longing to see for ages. Dress up in your finery, not because you are going somewhere. Do it because you can. Have fun with it. Wear the expensive dress that has been sitting in your wardrobe for ages, waiting for the 'right' occasion. Wear it while grocery shopping, or on the school run. The decadence of it will put a smile on your face, and it will infuse some giddy energy into your soul. Have your face painted, and transform yourself into a butterfly or a lioness. Go to a playground and allow yourself to fly high on the swings.

If it has been a long time since you engaged in peripheral soul nurturing, a good place to start can be with your teenage years. Think about the hobbies you used to do, or the things that you used to enjoy that have fallen by the wayside. Rediscover the things that you feel too old or grown up for. Thinking about them may inspire you to come up with some new ideas. The key to peripheral soul nurturing is to play with it. Have fun, and try not to take yourself too seriously.

Principle nurturing is an ongoing process. There is an interconnectedness between your soul's purpose and your joy. If you are in alignment with your soul's purpose it gives you joy, and if you do what gives you joy it will lead you to your soul's purpose. One follows the other.

Teaching has always given me joy. That does not mean that it came easy to me. Initially, I had to learn patience, and understand that not everyone learns at the same pace that I do. I had to lose my arrogance, and learn that, because I think something is amazing, it doesn't mean it will resonate with, or work for, someone else. I had to learn humility, and come to understand that behind each person there is a gentle soul that is reaching out. I had to learn to honour my own wisdom and trust what was in my heart.

I also had to learn to have fun. I learnt my craft from some amazing teachers, but in the early days I tried to emulate them. I tried to do things the way they did, and while I may have been competent and professional, it wasn't me. Over time I have learned to let my own light shine. I have embraced my own wisdom, and found my own way of teaching. I now play to my strengths, and I have stopped trying to be like someone else. I have learned that I need to teach what I believe in. This sometimes means turning down a pay check, to stay true to my heart.

I have learned that I connect much better with adults than I do with children or teenagers, so I refer that work to wonderful souls with whom working with young people allows their light to shine. And I have learned that engaging in my own process of growth provides me with the tools and the compassion to help others.

I did not know that teaching was my purpose. It evolved over time. If someone said to me ten years ago that I would be teaching women about womanhood, it would have seemed incomprehensible to me. What got me to this point was principle soul nurturing. When I worked as a psychic, lots of clients asked me how they could connect with their own guides.

I held my first holistic workshop to help people connect to their intuition. I was nervous, but as the day went on, I felt amazing. I remember thinking that I would love to do this all the time. It didn't feel anything like work to me. I was fuelled by the workshop, and I was on a high for days afterwards. From there I went on to teach people about shamanism, and the Goddess, and that road finally brought me to where I am today; teaching women about womanhood.

Yet I needed to experience every step of my life journey, the hurts and the joys, so that I could get to this point. Sometimes under our biggest hurt or issue lies the essence of our soul purpose. We need to integrate it, so that we can take the next step in our journey.

We often think our purpose in life will knock on our door and announce itself. Then we will be catapulted to success. That is not the case, and that is why principal soul nurturing is so important. Principle soul nurturing is your guide to your purpose. Do what gives you joy, and the rest will unfold. We sit around waiting to find out what our purpose is, in the hope that, once we figure it out, life can start, and we will be joyful and abundant. It doesn't happen that way.

I had been giving motivational talks long before I entered the world of complementary healing. It always gave me joy, but I knew that I was missing a piece of the puzzle. I kept doing it because, even though I felt something was missing, it fed my soul. Years later, I finally combined my skills as a motivator, healer, psychic, and student of tantra, to give workshops, and share what I had learned. The missing piece of the puzzle fell into place, and I knew in my heart that I had found my purpose. I really believe that all the years up to that point were my training ground, and for each one of those moments I am truly grateful because I would not be the woman I am now without them.

For you, principle soul nurturing may revolve around being a mum, a cleaner, a receptionist, a decorator, a coach, or a cook. It doesn't have to be grandiose, but if your heart lights up when you do it, you know you are on track. It is not necessarily something you automatically make a living from, but it is something that you would do without pay because you love it so much.

I have met people who work in a job that allows them to pay the bills, but more importantly their work schedule provides them with ample free time where they can pursue their principle soul nurturing. The energy this infuses them with is carried back into their job, and all their colleagues benefit from being in the presence of someone who is consciously engaging in principle soul nurturing.

In time, if you follow your joy, your principle soul nurturing will guide you to your soul's purpose. The secret to this process, however, is that you must follow your joy for joys sake, not because of where it may take you. If you have a preconceived idea of where your joy may lead, you immediately limit the opportunities and adventures that the universe may wish to place in your path. Open your heart to your joy, and allow your peripheral and principle soul nurturing to direct your path in life.

If painting gives you joy, firstly engage in some peripheral soul nurturing. You may go to a gallery to immerse yourself in the energy of art. If you like painting landscapes, take a walk in nature, and enjoy absorbing the energy of the outdoors. If you like painting people, hang out in a public place, and enjoy doing some people watching. Do your principle soul nurturing, get some paint, and put it on canvas.

Don't wait until you feel that you are good enough. Go ahead and do it. It takes time and practice to develop your craft and your own style, but you will never achieve that by sitting, staring at a canvas. Even if it is finger painting, it's a start. Paint, have fun, and then share your creation with someone loving and supportive. Once you start to engage in the energy of joy it will guide you to your next step.

If cooking gives you joy, prepare some delicious food. Allow it to awaken your taste buds. Take a trip to a farmers market and discover new ingredients. Buy a recipe book, and then use it! Create something, and then share it. The greatest joy comes from sharing something we have put our heart and our joy into. The more we share our joy the more it fuels us, and it inspires us to keep going. When you share what is in your heart, it can be witnessed, and the universe knows that you are committed to your purpose. It will willingly support you on every step of your journey.

Sometimes we are fearful of sharing, as we feel that we will be judged. This is where all your lovely feminine intuition comes to your aid. Allow your intuition to guide you as to who could nurture you in your process. I call these people 'Earth Angels'. They encourage us to step beyond our own limitations and self doubt, so that our light can shine. When you open your heart, and share your joy with another, you may be allowing someone whose purpose in life is to be an Earth Angel to follow her joy. And thus, in nurturing your soul, you allow someone else to nurture theirs.

Nurture, in its essence, is a feminine energy. The essence of the masculine is to protect. On occasion, the roles do swap, but if you are constantly in a state of protection, you are living your life from a place of the masculine. The more you nurture yourself the more you connect to the essence of your femininity, and the more you allow yourself to blossom as a woman.

Many women are excellent at nurturing others, but at this point of your journey you must turn your attention to nurturing yourself. Self-nurturing allows you to become energised with your life force, so that you exude your potential, and radiate to the world. You become a beacon of light that attracts all that is necessary to manifest your soul's purpose into your environment. Nurture yourself, and it automatically feeds your soul.

It doesn't matter if you are single or in a relationship, straight or gay. As women, we need to specifically nurture the essence of our womanhood. That's what gives us our fizz. It puts a sparkle in our eyes, and makes us feel sexy and desirable. It is not about being desirable for others, although that is a guaranteed by product of this aspect of nurturing. Instead, it is about becoming desirable to yourself. It's time, ladies, to light your own inner fire, and stir your juices, instead of waiting for another to do it for you. I can already feel some of you getting nervous, and raising your eyes up to heaven, but trust me on this one ladies, you have come this far. Let us journey together into the garden another little bit.

As women, many of us have become detached from our sexuality. In a world where there are so many mixed messages about sex and being sexy, it is sometimes difficult to find your sense of self among it all. Magazines that tell us about the latest look, or multiple orgasms, often leave us feeling inadequate instead of inspired. We believe that if we have children, or if we are in a long term relationship, or if we go beyond a certain age, it is natural for our sexual energy to diminish. This does not have to be the case.

Sexual energy is one of the most powerful internal forces available to you. Using your sexual energy to fertilise your garden can infuse you with new life. It has the ability to cleanse your cells, boost your immune system, increase your radiance, and most essentially it feels really good. I know that many people have a negative association to sex. I would ask you, however, at this juncture to separate the act of sex from sexual energy.

Sexual energy, in its purest form, is a powerful raw energy that lives within you. Some yogic traditions describe it as a coiled serpent (kundalini) that lives in the base of your spine, which, when awakened, opens energy pathways along your spinal chord. It initiates the flow of life force energy through your body. This energy is both transformative and nurturing. If you wish to fully awaken your kundalini it is advisable to do so with a teacher trained in kundalini yoga or tantra. For our purposes we are merely going to court the energy, and use it to awaken your inner seductress, so that she can nurture you.

Exercise – The Inner Seductress

Think back to earlier on our journey; to where we met our Yoni, our sacred centre of womanhood. Let us now reconnect with her once again. Remember, energy follows intent. By using our intention, and our breath, we can infuse our yoni with kundalini energy.

- Breathe into your yoni, and with each breath invite the kundalini energy to come into your sacred space. As you relax into the energy you may feel yourself get warm, excited, or even turned on.
- Imagine that the energy in your sacred space takes the form of a woman; your inner seductress. What does she look like? What is she wearing? Is she in heels, or

is she barefoot? How does she carry her body? How does she walk? What is her fragrance? Is she wearing make up? Does she use lipstick, or lip gloss?

• Take some time to really get a sense of her, and when you are ready allow her energy to merge with yours. How does that feel?

• When you are ready take a few breaths, and centre yourself.

Now it is time to play. Put together your seductress wardrobe. This may take a day or two, or perhaps you already have everything you need. Gather together all that you need to recreate the seductress you saw in your vision. Set aside some time when you won't be disturbed. You may want to start by having a shower or a bubble bath, and applying some sensual body lotion. Invoke the energy of your yoni, and the Goddess of Seduction. Find your own words, but you may wish to use something like this ...

> *"Juicy Yoni, please awaken, and unveil my life force, and my inner seductress, to me."*
>
> *"Sacred space of womanhood that dwells within me, unleash my fire."*
>
> *"Divine Goddess, show me the way so that I may nurture my soul."*

"Delicious Diva, reveal yourself to me, so that I may find my fizz."

Here is where the fun really starts. Dress yourself up as your inner seductress. You are not doing this for anyone else, only for yourself. Experience how it feels. Go beyond any resistance, and when you are dressed up (or dressed down as the case may be), strut your stuff. Pout your lips, take a walk across the room, and allow your kundalini energy, and your inner seductress, to move your body. Put on some music, and seduce yourself with dance.

Keep breathing into your yoni, all the time drawing the kundalini energy up into your body. Be open to how it feels. There is no wrong way, and no right way, to do this. Breathe past any old programming, or feelings of shame, or guilt about your body, and simply enjoy. Caress yourself, taste your lips, stroke the nape of your neck, and allow your body to come alive with life force. Have fun, and let your date with yourself nourish and nurture the woman that lives within.

You may wish to finish by pleasuring yourself, or you may wish to simply bask in the energy. Whatever you choose is perfect. When you are finished thank your yoni, and the Goddess of Seduction, for their loving guidance and support. Know that this energy lives within you, and once you connect with it you can call on it whenever and wherever you choose.

Nurturing is delicious in its exquisiteness. It feeds the depths of your soul. The more you nurture yourself, the more you grow and blossom. And the more radiant you become. Nurture yourself as a soul taking a journey in this lifetime, knowing that each time you nurture yourself, you align yourself to the essence of who you are. Nurture yourself as a woman so that you can bask in the divine radiance of the Goddess that is your birthright. Nurture, so that you can journey home, to yourself.

Exercise – Meeting the Creatrix

This is one of my favourite exercises. For me, it encapsulates so many different aspects of womanhood (love, nurturing, abundance, sexuality, and creativity). Each time I do it I deepen my connection to myself as a woman, and to my ability to manifest. It also frequently brings surprises! This exercise is designed to use the nurturing energy you have been working with, in its different forms, to nurture yourself at a deep level. It also heals any blocks that might be holding you back from your purpose.

The Creatrix is the creative energy that lives inside each and every woman. She is the energy that brought the world into being. She is the force that brings new life. She is all nurturing, and all sustaining. She is also the bringer of death to old soul parts that no longer serve you, so that they can be born anew. She is the mother, the crone, and the maid that you meet at the beginning of your life journey. She is all, and she is nothing, for she dwells in the depth of the internal void.

- Sit or lie comfortably.
- Place your hands over your tummy.
- Take some lovely deep breaths into your womb space; your creative centre. This is where the Creatrix lives within you.
- As you breathe, start to visualize a black void that fills your entire womb.
- Notice that this void has its own pulse and its own rhythm.
- Take some time to become familiar with the blackness, and be aware of any sensations you feel in your body.
- Call on the energy of the Creatrix to guide you.
- Visualise an aspect of your life that needs nurturing, and bring it into the void that is contained within your womb.
- You may wish to visualise your physical body, your emotional body, your sexual body, a project that you are working on, your finances, or one of your relationships, etc.
- Keep breathing into your womb space, and into the

energy that is contained within it, until you feel like you are heavily pregnant.

- When you are ready, visualise this energy passing from the womb down into the birth canal, and visualise it being birthed anew into the world.
- Take some time to rest in this energy, noticing your breathing, and any sensations that you may have.
- Thank the Creatrix for her help and guidance.
- Take a few deep breaths, and when you are ready, open your eyes, and bring your awareness back into the room where you are resting.
- Make some notes in your journal if you wish to do so.

You can repeat this exercise frequently for different areas of your life that you would like to nurture.

The Eighth Stepping Stone
~ Remember ~

"*Remember who you are. Since time began, story telling has been a fundamental core value in all tribal communities. Stories were told not just to entertain but to teach. It is much easier to remember a teaching if it is conveyed with the drama and ceremony that a true storyteller can bring to a tale. Stories were taught about hunting, raising children, honouring 'Mother Father God'. They taught the tribe about growing crops, giving birth, and dying. There were stories of great warriors, healers and magicians who had once been part of the tribe.*

Every story held an energy. Each energy helped awaken a part in the listener. It allowed them to remember the essence of who they were, and their connection to the tribe, to Spirit, and to the

Whole. Find your stories and remember. Talk to women about womanhood. Find books that resonate to your essence, and allow them to unlock a part of you that has been hidden and shut. Don't just look for fodder that will bring out your radiant self. Look for material that unveils your darker side. For unveiling the dark allows the influx of light, and the part of you that has been hiding in the shadows can then be reborn."

The journey to wholeness is a journey of remembering, where we claim back those parts of ourselves that have been dismembered over time. In shamanism, this is called soul retrieval, where we claim back a soul part that has been lost or damaged along the way. There are many reasons why we become dismembered. It can be as a result of a trauma, where we sacrifice a part of our essential self so that we will be safe or protected. In some instances we surrender a soul part so that we will be accepted.

For example, many young women surrender that sensual, sexual part of themselves, because they are told that it is dirty, or unacceptable. We slice off that part of our essence, so that we can remain within the safety of our tribe/family. Yet most women, when they talk about the day that they decided to surrender or tone down their sexuality, will tell you that, "I felt like a part of me died that day."

It didn't die. It merely separated from you, waiting

patiently until you were ready to call it back home. Similarly, women who have been sexually assaulted often surrender an aspect of their psyche, as the pain and trauma associated with it are so great. This may be a difficult concept to grasp, especially if you have experienced a violent sexual act, but it is important to separate the violation from the energy that was used to carry it out.

When a perpetrator carries out a sexual attack, there are two elements involved. The first is the attack on another human being. An attack of any sort, whether with a gun, fists, knife, or words, is incredibly traumatic. Now combine that assault with sexual energy, which is the most powerful creative force available to man. This energy is mutated to be a tool of destruction and pain, instead of creation and pleasure. One of the reasons why sexual assault is so traumatic to the victim is because at a soul level we know that sexual energy is the energy of the Divine. The trauma of being wounded by an energy that we know as Divine causes our soul to fracture in order to take the impact of the shock.

There are other, perhaps less traumatic, reasons why we become dismembered. If you hear the same message often enough and believe it, you may experience a dismembering; "You're not good enough", for example. When you start to believe this, the soul part that is 'good enough' may leave until you are ready to reintegrate it.

Other examples include, "Women are weak", so the strong part of you gets lost; "I wanted a boy, a son", so the feminine leaves, and you become masculine; "Don't touch down there!" and the sacredness of your sex centre gets abandoned or hidden. And the list goes on.

Some of our dismemberings may not even be as a result of our own experiences. You may be carrying cultural or ancestral dismemberings which are impacting on your sense of self. In Ireland, for example, one of our cultural dismemberings is that sexuality and spirituality are separate. Sex is dirty, and spirituality is clean, so one is not acceptable in the presence of the other. As a nation, this has had a huge effect on our attitude to sex, and to ourselves as sexual beings. In tantra, on the other hand, sex is seen as a pathway to spiritual enlightenment. Sex is a way to experience oneness with the Divine, instead of a separation from our Divinity.

Sometimes we will know the exact moment when our soul part slipped away. Other times we have no conscious awareness of when it happened. Instead, what we have is an emptiness, or a void that dwells inside. Sometimes it is a longing, but you don't know for what. Sometimes it is a sadness that you can't explain, and sometimes it feels like an internal struggle between two contradictory parts of yourself. The Madonna and the Whore is a common struggle for women as we try to reconcile the sacred and the sexual within us. When we claim back the soul part that allows us to accept that we are both sacred and sexual, our inner conflict disappears.

On occasion, remembering can be difficult. You may feel dizzy, disorientated, and nauseated, as the old paradigm in which you have been constrained starts to crumble away. This will pass, and it will be replaced by the sweetness of the remembering experience. You may experience a sense of warmth, inner peace, or calm, and frequently tears. These may be joyous tears, as you release the pain of the past, and experience the sweetness of the soul part that has been waiting patiently for you so that it could return home. Each time we remember, some of the emptiness that lives inside us is replaced with a deeper knowing of who we are.

Complete remembering rarely happens all in one go. It would be too overwhelming for most of us. Each remembering is accompanied by a soul lesson. We need time to integrate these lessons so that we can weave them into the fabric of our being, and learn from them. Each remembering strengthens us and deepens our connection to ourselves.

There was a woman that I used to be very friendly with. She was a powerful woman in her own right, with an intoxicating whirlwind energy. That highly charged energy was great to be around until it was turned against you. I realised that over time I was afraid of this woman. To avoid the wrath of the whirlwind, I never stood up to her, even when I felt that she was wrong in a given situation. I abandoned my integrity, and my own sense of power, to keep the peace. After a difficult period of separation from her, I faced my fear of confrontation. I remembered the part of me that honoured my own wisdom and insight. I also honoured her for the lesson that I had learned as a result of our relationship.

Many months later I met another woman who had similar energy. This time, with my new deeper sense of self, I was able to enjoy this new woman's company while remaining centred in the essence of my being.

Remembering is a process. It is a journey home to ourselves. A remembering occurs when you are ready to take the next step along the path. Sometimes, it may occur spontaneously. You are struck by an instant heartfelt knowing. More often than not however it is triggered by an external stimulus. I can still recall how something inside me woke up when I read Jessie E. Ayani's, '*The Lineage of the Codes of Light*'. As I read passages of how women were honoured and initiated into womanhood, in beautiful heartfelt rituals, I started to cry. The part of me that was longing to be honoured as a woman remembered my sacredness and came home that day.

Connecting to the day when I realised as a woman how beautiful my yoni was still sends shivers down my spine. I took a hand mirror and fought the huge resistance within me. I felt shame because I wasn't really sure what I was looking at, and guilt for doing any of this in the first place. I parted my legs, and let all the guilt and the shame pass. Then I let the waves of revulsion pass. I kept looking, finding my clitoris in the folds, gazing at the softness, the moistness, and the difference in colour and texture.

And then magic happened. I remembered. I remembered all the beauty that dwelled within my sex. I remembered that this was a reflection of me, and that I too was beautiful. I remembered that I was deeply connected to this beautiful cavern of creation and pleasure. I remembered that this was the centre of my power as a woman. In honouring my sex, I honoured my power, my sacredness, and myself. I remembered and honoured that I was Divine. That remembering profoundly transformed me. It instilled a deep sense of aliveness within me, as well as a deep sense of inner beauty. In those moments I allowed myself to wake up to the essence of my being, and in doing so I changed the course of my life forever.

I know that for so many women, connecting to your physical body is difficult. We have been programmed not to touch ourselves 'down there'. Often our gynaecologist or our lover is more familiar with our sex centre than we are. Alternatively, if we do go 'down there' we feel that it has to be connected to sex. We rarely visit our yoni solely to rest in the energy of the sacred, and to be present with the Divine.

I have read many books and attended many workshops on my journey of discovery regarding womanhood. What I have learned is that there is a lot of beautiful information regarding the sacredness of the feminine, and all of it helps us to remember an aspect of our being. However, a lot of it is lacking one key element. If you truly want to step into your power as a woman, and feel that sacred energy in every cell of your being (feeling is a feminine energy), as opposed to knowing it as an intellectual concept (intellectualising is a masculine energy), you need to acquaint yourself with the wet, moist folds of your body. It may be painful at first. There may be tears and revulsion. There may be huge resistance and tantrums. But in time that will pass, and you will remember. You will remember that you are part of an ancient lineage; an ancient lineage of women who knew in their hearts, in their souls, and in their bodies, that they were Sacred.

Stories are a powerful healing tool, not only because they allow the listener to remember parts of themselves that have been lost, but also because they allow the listener to experience the darker aspects of the psyche. Our society no longer relishes the dark, but it is part of the natural cycle of nature. Day becomes night, and the brightness of spring and summer is naturally replaced by the darkness of autumn and winter.

We have come to see the dark as something to be feared, shunned, and hidden. Yet, in tribal cultures, and in many ancient mythologies, the descent into the darkness was an intrinsic part of the soul's journey. It is in the darkness we find our strengths, our gifts, and our courage. It is in the darkness that we are initiated so that we can emerge wiser, with the inner strength to take our place in the world. It is in the darkness that we often find our light. Many of us try to run away from that which we perceive to be our inner darkness. Yet the darkness is an intrinsic aspect of who we are, and when we don't honour it, it bleeds through into our everyday lives, causing havoc as it tries to demand our attention. We go into battle with the aspects of ourselves that we feel are less than desirable, instead of embracing them, so that they can reveal their gifts and strengths to us.

The depths of the shadow, and of the darkness, are where the most delectable part of us lives. Because we are often afraid of the dark, those parts never get fully explored, so their potential is never fully realised. Seeds germinate in the dark, and so too do the seeds of our soul. Most people only glance into the shadows, and as a result their perception of what awaits them in the darkness is mutated by their limited visibility.

To fully experience a remembering you must fully

experience in a safe way the darker aspects of the universal and individual psyche. To do this you can write a story from the perspective of a character you would least like to be, and see where the story meanders. See what parallels it instigates in relation to your own life.

The key to writing a story is to do so with no specific outcome in mind. You are merely providing an opportunity to unwind, and unravel the energy that is lurking in the darkness. This is not about writing prose. Do not concern yourself with grammar, punctuation, or seemingly unconnected sentences. Instead, you let the story lead you to wherever it needs to go. You are merely a channel, a voice for the part of you that has been waiting in the darkness.

Allow yourself to roll around in the energy, as if you were taking a mud bath. Don't worry about getting stuck there. If you surrender to the story, the story will surrender the healing gift, or new awareness, that is waiting for you. We only get stuck in the energy when we try to resist it. When we resist, it keeps clinging to us, demanding our attention. But when we embrace it, so that we can honour and celebrate it, we will be set free.

Story telling is fun. It is a wonderful way to delve into the hidden recesses of ourselves. Play with it. Go on an adventure with the selfish, greedy, impatient parts of yourself. See what happens when you meet your inner prostitute, tramp, or bitch. What are the gifts that belong to the unhappy mother, the frustrated wife, or the lonely executive? Be open to being surprised. In the darkness of the shadows lies a part of you waiting, in all its beauty, to be reborn.

The more we remember the more we come home to ourselves. The more we come home to ourselves the more we realise that we are not separate from our Divinity, but that we are part of the Divine. Our light and our darkness are all part of the whole. When we remember this without fear or judgement we come back into balance within ourselves. Allow yourself to be remembered, and you will remember that the lineage you come from is the womb of the Divine.

Exercise – Remembering

- Set aside some quiet time where you won't be disturbed.
- Take a few moments to breathe deeply into your body.
- As you breathe, invite any aspects of yourself that are ready to be remembered to make themselves available to you now.
- You may wish to set your intention, if there is one specific aspect of yourself that you would like to work with. For example, "Today I would like to tell the story of my inner slut."

- Using your journal, or a notepad, write "Once upon a time there was a beautiful young girl who lived in a really dark cave ..." at the top of a page.
- Without thinking about it, let your hand move across the page, and allow the rest of the story to be written.
- DO NOT self censor as you write.
- Don't judge or guess the words. Simply let the story unfold on the page before you.
- The story may be long or short, one page or many pages; it doesn't matter. Just allow it to take shape, and allow those parts of you that are ready to be remembered to come forward.
- When you are finished, spend some time in the energy of the story that has emerged, and allow it to unlock the parts of you that have been hidden away.
- You may wish to do something to honour the gift that you found in the darkness. Paint it, celebrate it with fresh flowers, spend some time in nature integrating it, write a poem about this new part of you, etc.
- Repeat this exercise every time you feel that you are ready to remember or rediscover another part of who you are.

Exercise – Remembering your Lineage.

- Sit or lie comfortably.
- Take a few deep breaths to centre yourself.
- Start to breathe into your womb, and into your sex.
- As you breathe, feel the beat of an ancient drum.
- Allow your imagination to carry you to the time and place where this drum was played.
- Notice that you are with other women. Where are you? In a forest, near the beach? Is it day time or night time? Is there a fire?
- Notice that you and the other women are dancing; a dance from long, long ago. These are the women of your soul lineage.
- As you dance they whisper to you. They whisper to you so that you can remember. They whisper your soul name. They whisper your gifts. They whisper the names of the healing herbs that you may have carried in your medicine bundle.
- They whisper everything you need to know, so that you can remember who you are. And all the time they dance a beautiful tribal dance.
- The music stops, and you see in front of you the Source of all Life and of all Creation. She walks towards you, and without words allows you to remember your ancient ancestry; the womb from where you were first birthed, your connection to the Divine.

- Take some time to enjoy this moment, breathing into the feelings, and the rememberings.
- When you are ready, thank all of these women from your heart for the gift they shared with you today, and know that you can return to meet them at any time.
- Taking some deep breaths, bring your awareness back into your room.
- Wiggle your feet and your hands to reconnect with your body, and allow yourself to rest in the energy of your remembering.

The Ninth Stepping Stone
⁓ *Honesty* ⁓

*"Y*ou *need to be honest with yourself about who you are. You are a child of God, but in that you are also unique. You are not who people expect you to be. That is why we get caught up in roles. We try to conform to what we think our family and friends want us to be, so that we are accepted and loved. Be yourself. Be true to yourself and be honest about your gifts, dreams, and potential. To paraphrase Marianne Williamson, "You are a child of God. You playing small does not serve the world."*

The world needs leaders, not followers. Not leaders who bring us to war, or to hate, or to greed. But leaders who stand solidly in their integrity, and shout to the world, "This is me, and I am beautiful. Look at me, and allow me to reflect your own inner beauty

to you." Because if we are honest, we can honestly see the beauty
in each soul, and we honestly know that we are not separate from
each other, or the Divine."

This has been quite a journey so far. We have come a
long way as we have followed the stepping stones down
into your Inner Garden. We have composted the past,
and stepped into the realm of the Divine Feminine.
We have met with our Awareness, so that she could
inform us of the aspects of our lives that are in need
of our attention. We stepped forward towards Self
Appreciation so that we could explore our woundings
as being wonderful opportunities for growth. We also
honoured our bodies as the incarnation of the Goddess.

We stepped towards Forgiveness, where we opened
our pipe to ourselves and others, so that we could set
ourselves free. The next stepping stone allowed us
to surrender to Love, so that we could deepen our
connection to ourselves, and to others. As the light
faded, we turned a corner into the domain of Death
where we said goodbye to those parts of ourselves that
were great teachers but now no longer serve us. The
darkness of death was replaced by the by the brightness
of Life, where we invited our Divine Essence to radiate
through us.

The next stepping stone invited us to Nurture our
delicious essence, so that we could blossom and grow.

Our blossoming allowed us to Remember the intrinsic soul parts of our being that had been lost or hidden along the way, so that we could be whole again.

Now we take another step. Reaching your foot forward, place it firmly on the stone of Honesty. This stone represents the truth that lies within you, so that you no longer have to hide from yourself, or from the world.

I have spent the longest time being afraid to be myself. I felt that I would be judged, that people couldn't handle me, that what I had to say was too 'out there'. Mostly these were all excuses. What I was really afraid of was owning my magnificence. I was afraid to admit to myself that I was a child of God, and a daughter of the Goddess. If I admitted that, then I had to honour that all parts of me, light and dark, were perfection incarnate, and that in each moment I was Divine. If I was Divine then I didn't need to keep waiting until I was fixed, and this would mean that there was nothing in the way of me being me.

I didn't need to take more courses, heal more wounds, or wait until my business was a huge success, to get on with my life. I simply needed to honour all aspects of my being, and get on with it. The idea of 'getting on with it' was more terrifying than being broken or wounded. Getting on with it required diligence, discipline, and dedication. It required me to focus on my soul's purpose, and not wade around in the waters of self doubt and pity. It required me to pay better attention to my diet and exercise program, so that I had the energy to do all the things I needed to do.

It required me to stop getting side tracked by all the 'woe is me' parts of my life. It required me to work with the energy of my own inner garden daily, so that I could be centred, informed, and juiced up. It required me to stop putting off doing the parts of my job that I wasn't so keen on, or competent at. It required me to be honest about my gifts and talents, but I also needed to be honest about my fear. What I was really afraid of was not that people couldn't handle me, but that the thought of owning and accepting my own beauty, passion, grace, and Divinity was overwhelming.

On our path to honesty, we must also be honest about the roles we assume. From early on we dress ourselves in different roles so that we will receive love. The joker, the A student, the sickly or needy child, or the drama queen, are a few examples. We learn that to get attention (i.e. love) we must do something to earn or attract it. Ideally, love is unconditional. We love each other because of who we are (Divinity), not because of what we are, or what we do. Unfortunately, our parents, in many cases, had lost their sense of Divinity before we arrived, so we respond to their woundings by adapting a role that will allow us to connect with them. This sets the stage for how we continue to engage with the world.

When we assume a role, we cease to be centred in our being; our essence. As women, we often sacrifice some of our delicious feminine energy, and become more masculine in the way we engage with the world. As we strive to prove ourselves we energetically grow balls, and compete with men as men. Then we often wonder why we cannot attract a strong masculine mate into our lives. This is difficult when we are the ones energetically, and literally, wearing the trousers.

Another way we can contort our feminine energy is to use it to manipulate those around us. We flatter them with our feminine charm, so that they can fulfil our needs. Men rarely stick around, as they get tired of being used and abused. If you don't fit into either of these two categories (and we all have a bit of each of them within us to a lesser or greater extent) chances are that you have assumed the role of the judge. The judge passes judgment over her sisters for their woundings and behaviours, and encourages others to do the same. She is often the office gossip. In reality, is it a clever role that she uses to deflect attention, or criticism, from herself.

When we act out from our roles, and there are hundreds of them, we fail to let the fullest expression of our light shine. This is why honesty is such a beautiful step. Honesty works in two ways. Firstly, a role is often so woven into our being that we don't even know we are doing it. At each interaction, either with ourselves or others, ask yourself, are you honestly feeling joy, pleasure, and grace? If the answer is 'no', and if you are feeling tired, frustrated, depressed, or annoyed, chances are that you are living your life through one of your many roles.

Roles take a lot of energy, as we are constantly trying to be something that we are not. We are also suppressing ourselves from being our potential. This doesn't mean that you cannot be successful in business, or that you cannot be sensual or wise. But in doing so you express those aspects of your essence from being centred in your womanhood, as apposed to being centred in your woundings.

One of my roles was the strong independent woman. I used it to camouflage my weaknesses and insecurities. I wore this role like a bullet proof jacket. It protected me, and allowed nothing to penetrate. It also, on many occasions, left me isolated and alone. I was like a closed book that only a chosen few knew the contents of. I often appeared unapproachable, when in reality I was incredibly scared.

As I embraced my femininity I had to say goodbye to Ms. Strong Independence. In her place arrived Ms. Sensitive Receiving. I learned to walk with my gifts and vulnerabilities in the world, and receive support in all aspects of my life along the way. The transition was terrifying. I felt raw, vulnerable, and completely exposed.

All the time I knew the 'me' that was emerging was a more honest expression of my essence. Once I took ownership of my sensitivity, and allowed myself to receive, it was like I could finally relax my shoulders and take a breath. Ms. Strong Independence was high maintenance. Her protective shield sucked from my life force, and ultimately she left me exhausted.

The second beautiful aspect of honesty with regard to roles is that once you honestly acknowledge them, you allow yourself to access the gift that is contained within them. Each role contains a golden nugget of your essence that has been hidden underneath your wounding. By gathering the nuggets we can string together the precious components of who we are, and live a life based on the authenticity of our being. The gift of Ms. Strong Independence was her strength. Instead of using it to protect myself, and keep others at a distance, I was able to use her strength to stand tall in my sensitivity, and be more open. When we are honest about our roles we allow our inner compass to naturally reset itself, and we become more aligned to the Divinity that dwells within.

The next part of honesty that I invite you to embrace is being honest about your feelings. As women, we are naturally emotive. We are often taught to suppress our feelings, or keep them bottled up, so that we don't cause a scene, or embarrass others. This usually results in an outpouring of emotion when we can't contain ourselves anymore, or depression as we push our feelings further and further away from the surface. This stagnation and blocking of feelings separates us from our essence. As we honour how we are feeling, we become a crystal conduit for our essence to flow through, instead of a blocked sewage pipe.

As you start to honour your feelings you will experience an integral aspect of womanhood. You will experience the fluidity of your feelings and emotions as they wash through your body. You may be happy in this moment, and sad in the next. You may even be both at the same time. This is not unnatural, unusual, or dishonest. Allow the feelings to wash through you, and honour each of them.

Don't get hung up on holding onto what you perceive to be positive feelings, and rush past the negative ones. Each feeling brings its own experience, and the gift of womanhood is that you can experience all of them, and allow them to nourish you in different ways. Having a good cry is equally as important as having a good belly laugh. Find the pleasure in both. The more honest you are about your feelings, the more you connect to you truth, and the more you allow your essence to blossom and flourish.

With each new emotion simply say, "Welcome. I honour you, and I honour that I am feeling _____ _____" (happy, sad, angry, excited, nervous, turned on, etc.) Allow the energy to flood your being, and then allow it to wash through you, enjoying the experience as it does so. In time, you will come to enjoy and take pleasure in the infinite array of emotions that you are able to feel, whether you deem them to be positive or negative. The more you feel, the more expansive you allow your essence to become.

An important aspect of honesty is to honour your truth in each moment. This can be as simple as honestly stating what you desire to eat, or which movie you would like to see in the presence of others. Honesty is like a muscle. The more we exercise, it the easier it becomes to express our truth. That way when we need to source our truth from within, for the bigger decisions in life, we know how to connect with it.

When my ex-husband asked me to marry him, something went 'ping' inside me. It only lasted perhaps a nanosecond, and I purposely paid no attention to it. What I learned many years later, was that this was my truth. It was trying to get my attention, to allow me to give voice to the tiniest spark of doubt and uncertainty that lived within me. But I ignored it, and the rest, as you know, is history.

I am not so blasé about my truth anymore. The more I practice listening to it, and voicing it, the more I grow and step fully into the essence of who I am. We often avoid being honest in case it upsets or hurts others.

What we mean when we say this is that, "I'm afraid that I won't be loved if I am honest about how I am feeling."

Express your truth from your heart. This is an honest expression of where you are at in that moment. It takes courage and practice, but the more you do it the more you will set yourself free from the constraints of the past. The gorgeous man in my life recently mentioned to me about how he would like us to get married. My whole being started to spiral into chaos, but I smiled and said nothing. I already had one failed marriage behind me. My pride wouldn't allow me to risk another. What would my family think if I got married again? How would they feel if I failed again? Did I love him enough to marry him? And on and on I went.

I bottled all this up for a day or two, but my awareness prompted me that I was being dishonest with him about how I was feeling. So from my heart I expressed my fears and doubts, and how, by telling him that I was afraid, he would love me less. He listened, and held me in his arms without judgement, and let this hodgepodge of energy unwind from my being.

Over the next few days something beautiful happened. All my fears and doubts and stubborn pride evaporated, and I came to a new place of truth in my being. I was truthfully and honestly head over heels in love with this man. My fears and confusion were honest in that moment, and by expressing them I was able to allow them to wash through me, so that a deeper truth could be unveiled.

When we are honest about how we are feeling, we provide ourselves with a beautiful opportunity to birth all the emotional energy that is spiralling around inside us. Up until that point the energy is formless, and usually it takes up a huge amount of space in our mind, and in our body, as we try to contain it. When we birth it we give it form, and allow it to be witnessed. In witnessing the energy we can clearly see what we are dealing with, and we can allow ourselves to step further into our truth.

I was caught in the spiral of formless energy that was within me regarding getting married again. When I birthed it, I could see my fears, my desires, and my truth. I was able to acknowledge and honour the fear, and also witness that, even though I was fearful, I loved this man deeply. To birth this energy you can lend your voice to it; paint it, sing it, dance it, or write it out of your being. Choose a format that will allow the energy to flow through you, so that it can be witnessed by yourself or by someone with whom you may wish to share it.

I know that when it comes to honesty some people feel like they have to atone for their actions in the past. I do not prescribe to this particular school of thought. I feel that these are often the actions of someone filled with regret and remorse, and that they take this course of action to make only themselves feel better.

Time is considered by many to be linear. It's comprised of the past, present and future. Often, the modern therapy model is based on the principle that, if you wish to heal something that you have become aware of in the present, then you need to return to the past where the wounding occurred. Then you need to heal it, so that your future will be different. In the shamanic model we see time as non linear. Imagine that you are the pebble that is dropped into the pond. The ripples that are generated as a result filter out in all directions.

In shamanism if you heal in the present time you become the pebble in the pond, and the effects of your healing ripple out in all directions. The effects of healing in the present moment are felt simultaneously in the 'past' and in the 'future'. Many of us get caught up in trying to heal our parents, our partner, or our siblings. We don't need to. Nor is it our responsibility. We often get caught up in trying to fix others because it is a welcome distraction from having to immerse ourselves in our own healing journey. All we need to do is heal ourselves so that we are centred in our Divinity, and the ripple effect will take care of the rest. Please do not engage in your own healing because you have a desired outcome for how that will affect others. Remember, your perception of healing might be different to that of the Universe. So "Let go and let God", as the saying goes.

As we set ourselves free from our roles, and become

a beautiful crystal conduit for our feelings, the truth and honesty of who we are begins to emerge. The Universe then provides us with an opportunity in each moment to stand in our honesty. Are the clothes we wear an honest reflection of who we are? Is the food you eat and honest reflection of the vibration you wish to hold in your body? Is the work we do an honest expression of our passions and talents? Are the opinions we voice an honest articulation of our beliefs? Are you an honest expression of your essence while in the company of people who challenge you the most?

There is no point in dwelling in the past about all the times that you were not honest. Instead, understand that the time to be honest is right here, right now in the present moment. Every fresh new moment from this point forward provides you with an opportunity to stand tall in your honesty, and be who you came here to be. You have the ability to birth yourself, and be witnessed in each new moment of each new day. In doing so you are able to deepen your connection with yourself, and become intimate with your essence.

If you are being honest with yourself, you have to stop playing small. To be the fullness of your essence you need to be honest about your gifts, and honour each beautiful one of them. When I was growing up we quickly learned not to be 'big headed'. In other words you were not supposed to go around telling yourself, or others, how great you were. If by chance someone did notice your greatness, and paid you a compliment, you also learned how to rebuff the compliment. This guaranteed there was no possible opportunity for you to feel good about your self; "What a gorgeous dress you're wearing", "What, this old thing? I have it for ages", "You did an amazing job", "Thanks. I just did what I get paid for", "You have a gorgeous singing voice", "Oh, you should hear my sisters, they are so much better than I am."

And on and on it goes. So my lovelies, it's time to get honest about your gifts, talents, and wonderfulness. Firstly you need to admit to yourself how great you are. Wherever you are reading this now, take a moment to sit up straight. Take a breath, and start to list out all your amazing qualities and talents. This may be really uncomfortable at first, but remember that you are exercising your 'honesty muscle'.

Also remember that by expressing your gifts you birth them, and give them form. There is no point having the best singing, mothering, or entrepreneurial talent, for example, if are unwilling to give it form. This only facilitates you keeping your light firmly hidden under a bushel, and trust me, no one including you benefits from that.

Take a few moments each and every day to tell yourself how amazing you are. Very soon you will start to believe your own publicity. Not because you are faking it, but because it is true. It is hard to play small when you realise, and honour, your greatness. The next stage of this process is allowing yourself to embrace each and every compliment that comes your way. Compliments are a beautiful gift bestowed to us so that we can honour our greatness and our beauty.

When we refuse to accept a compliment it's like taking someone's carefully chosen gift and smashing it to the floor. When you are gifted a compliment, take a moment to look the bearer directly in the eye; smile and say "Thank you." In doing so you receive the gift that they have presented to you, and you allow yourself to honestly acknowledge a beautiful aspect of your being. Compliments should not be something that we crave to feed our neediness and our lack of self worth. If this is the case we need to get honest about why we require external validation. A compliment should be something that allows you to deepen your connection to your magnificence. Compliments should allow you to ultimately receive yourself.

For the longest time people would pay me compliments, and because I was so good at dismissing them I eventually started to feel that they were talking about someone else. It was like the compliment couldn't permeate the 'I won't be big headed' force field that I had created. I wasn't able to take ownership of the compliment, or be honest about my gifts. I have found this to be the case for many women. If you would like to dismantle your force field, and if you are really ready to embrace your greatness, this is what you have to do. Start complimenting yourself!

You can compliment yourself on anything and everything; from getting out of bed in the morning, to doing the laundry, to securing a new client, or receiving a big juicy bonus at work. Have fun with it. Try to find a compliment in even the smallest of actions, and see how it transforms how you feel about yourself. Once you start to acknowledge your greatness you will find that others start to do so as well. At first it will feel strange, and perhaps unsettling, as your force field begins to shatter. In time however you will start to glow. You will glow with your radiance. And you will glow as the honesty of who you are starts to filter through your being. You will start to stand tall like a beautiful sunflower with your face held high to the sun; resplendent and radiant for all to see.

Be warned that as soon as we start to compliment ourselves our self sabotaging mechanism starts to kick in. It's like having two voices in your head; the 'I'm amazing' voice, and the 'I'm so worthless' voice. Be honest that you can feel both ways about yourself at the same time. Also, honour both these aspects of yourself. Remember that both of them contain a gift that you can embrace. Don't try to suppress the voice which you perceive to be negative. This takes far too much energy. Instead, court it, give it form, and birth it. That way you can witness it, and honestly decide if it is a belief that you would like to hold on to, or let go.

And now my beauties, we come to the delicious cherry on the honesty cake. I know this is going to be difficult for some of you to digest, but here is the most honest thing that I can tell you. You, beautiful lady, are a child of God. If you can receive this, and allow this to permeate your being, you will know from the depth of your being that you are Divine. You are the incarnation of the love between the God and the Goddess. You are divinity, you are perfection, and you are whole.

You are whole, even in your woundings. You were never separate from the Divine, even in your darkest hour, as you are the Divine incarnate. You are an intrinsic part of all that is, all that ever was, and all that has yet to come. You are part of a lineage of women, birthed from the womb of the Goddess. You are not simply tending to your garden, you are the garden. Can you breathe this in? Can you allow yourself to receive the honest beauty of who you are? Rest in that; the joy, the sadness, the frustration, the excitement, and the contradiction. On this journey towards wholeness, it is time to honestly remember that you were never cast out of the garden. You were, in fact, the garden all along.

The world needs leaders, not followers. By honouring your gifts, your beauty, and your sacred Divinity, you light the way for others to follow. Being honest allows others to do the same, and we become role models, where we lift each other up instead of tearing each other down. We create a sisterhood based on giving and receiving in equal amounts from our hearts, not from our wounds. We sit side by side, and honour the Divine beauty that lives within each of us. We honour our imperfections, knowing that they are our greatest gifts and teachers. We relish the rawness that we feel on the path to wholeness as we accept that our rawness creates the space for our authentic self to come forward. We do not allow each other to wallow in our limitations. Instead, we encourage each other to grow and stretch. And we are honest in our remembering of the Greatness of who we are. We are the garden, and we are the fertile soil where others can sow their seeds so that they too can flourish. This is the essence of Woman.

Exercise – The honesty muscle training program.

- Make a list, write a poem, paint a picture, or create a collage that honours your gifts and talents. Think of it as a celebration of your essence. Share it with people who you know will be supportive, so that they can witness the birthing of your radiance.

- Compliment yourself frequently throughout the day, even for the smallest of tasks.
- Learn to receive compliments. Look the bearer in the eye, smile, and graciously say "Thank you."
- Start to pay honest compliments to anyone and everyone that you meet during the day. It could be the lady serving you coffee, the mail man, your boss, your kids, or your lover. It may feel awkward at first, but as you exercise your honesty muscle it will become a superbly enjoyable part of your day.
- Buy or gather a gorgeous bouquet of flowers that is an honest reflection of your Divine Inner Garden, including your contradictions. Give it pride of place in your home; preferably somewhere that you will see it often. Allow the variety of colours and textures to remind you that there are many parts to your essence, and that they are all an honest reflection of who you are.

The Tenth Stepping Stone
～ *Celebration* ～

"If you embrace the other principles, you must celebrate. Life is a wondrous, joyous gift. Celebrate that you are alive, that you are living a life of love and truth, and allow every single thing that you do each day to be a celebration of that. Do not celebrate low key. Allow the world to witness the avalanche of beauty and love that pours forth from you in each moment.

God celebrates with the seasons. He has so much colour and radiance and beauty to show the world. He must have seasons so that He can change the palette of creation. Celebrate your inner palette. Allow it to light up the world.

If you were a garden of potential what kind of garden would you be? A lush tropical paradise, a cottage garden with dainty, sun-kissed flowers? A wild herbaceous border? Whatever your colour, whatever your garden, now is your time to express it, and share it with the world."

Aren't women the most amazing creatures? We are wise, sensual, intuitive, nurturing, caring, powerful, abundant, radiant, and delicious. Should we not celebrate that? Nowadays, celebrations are often reserved for what we deem to be 'special occasions'. What is more special than you?

Celebration is the art of finding the sacred in each moment. Every time we celebrate, we connect ourselves not only to our own divinity but to all that is, in whatever form that takes for you. It could be the Goddess, God, Spirit, etc. It is an opportunity to witness yourself in an engagement with the sacred. In celebrating, you root yourself firmly in your Divine essence.

In tribal communities, celebrations accompanied rites of passage. They marked not only a physical transformation but a psychological transformation within the individual. They were an opportunity, facilitated and supported by the tribe, to honour your passage from one stage of life to another. A celebration helps to anchor the experience into your body. It also allows you the opportunity to take the next step on this journey called life.

We are often afraid of celebration. What if people

think we are being arrogant or big headed, because we are celebrating something 'small'? This is not your concern. Your concern is to honour each precious moment, and the sacredness contained within it. Even if you are having what you perceive to be the most awful day, celebrate it! In doing so, you connect yourself to your Divinity. The wisdom contained within the situation will unfold, and you will (trust me on this) provide yourself with a previously unthought-of idea to move forward.

Celebration is one of the cornerstones of our existence. Without it we become numb to the possibilities available to us. Celebration anchors us firmly in the now. Celebration allows us to lift the consciousness of all present, to create sacred moments where we commune with the Divine. This doesn't mean that celebrations have to be zealous, sombre affairs. They are what they are; celebratory. Kick up your heels, have some fun, do things you wouldn't normally do, and enjoy them.

Celebration is one of the most enjoyable ways to expand your consciousness, and nurture your essence. Celebration is like champagne bubbles for your soul. It fizzes you up, makes you intoxicated with your own deliciousness, and is most definitely contagious. When you entered the garden, you composted the rot and decay in your life. Then you nurtured yourself, and in doing so you allowed yourself to blossom as a beautiful woman. Celebrate the journey that you have taken, and continue to celebrate it every step of the way.

Life is such a wonderful gift. We often only value it when it is almost taken away from us, or when we lose a loved one. Don't wait until you are threatened with the loss of life before you start celebrating its exquisiteness. Celebrate that you got out of bed this morning, because this means that you are available for many new opportunities and experiences. If you did not get out of bed, celebrate that you are resting, and nurturing your physical body.

Do not get hung up on only one aspect of celebration. Find as many different ways as possible to celebrate yourself throughout the day. Your coffee break could be transformed from a quick ten minute time out to a celebration of all the work you have done so far that day. Celebrate your Greatness. If you do not, no one else will.

When you start to celebrate yourself, amazing things start to happen. You become fun to be around. People want you at their party because you *are* the party. Have fun, enjoy yourself, and remember to celebrate your delicious magnificence every single step of the way. What is the point of spending long days tending to your garden if you don't ever take the time to sit and bask in the beauty that you have created?

Celebrate each time you gain a new insight into

yourself as a woman. Celebrate when you let go of something that doesn't need to be part of your life anymore. It could be an item of clothing, a relationship, or a belief. When one of my friends got divorced she had a party. For her it was a way to honour the time she had with her ex-husband, and the child that they were blessed with. It was also a wonderful opportunity to celebrate the new phase of her life that she was stepping into, and have it witnessed by her friends.

When we don't celebrate, life quickly becomes mundane, as there is then an absence of the sacred. You are a Divine being, and the more you celebrate yourself, the more you radiate with Divinity, and the more irresistible you become. Right up until my late twenties I was quite shy. I didn't mind talking to people on a one to one basis, but if I had to go anywhere on my own, especially if it was work related, where I wouldn't know any of the other guests, I would be terrified. As a result, I would retreat into myself, and wait for the first available, and polite, opportunity to leave. I must have appeared either arrogantly aloof, or nervously agitated.

It's hardly any surprise that people would rarely talk to me. If, by some lucky twist of fate, someone did speak to me I would stick to them like a limpet for the evening, terrified that they might leave and I would be on my own again. I spent many evenings with people who at the time I considered to be incredibly boring, so I wouldn't be on my own. Thankfully, I learned how to celebrate myself, and it changed my life. Now, whether I am going out to a function on my own or with company, I celebrate myself. I celebrate whatever I am feeling in the moment, and allow it to fizz up through me.

If I am feeling insecure or uncomfortable, I stand firmly in it, and repeat something like this to myself, "I am really amazing for coming to this party. I am so fabulous for coming to an event that allows me to grow and stretch through my insecurity. I celebrate my courage and my strength. I am so damn gorgeous in my vulnerability that every single person here longs to talk to me." Guess what happens; people talk to me, I talk to people, I dance, I celebrate, and I have so much fun. I also celebrate each person who speaks to me; "Thank you so much for taking the time to talk to me. It was really lovely."

What I have realised is that by and large we are all the same. We are all insecure in some aspect of our life. The person I thought of as boring years ago was probably as terrified, or as uncomfortable, as I was. I also consciously celebrate when I feel confident, radiant, or sexy. Celebration, however you choose to do it, creates a space where you can experience the divine essence of yourself and others in a fun and joyous way. It is infinitely more fun to celebrate my vulnerability and see the blessing in that, than to berate myself for not being good enough. Berating ourselves makes us small, and causes our essence to shrink. Celebrating ourselves and others allows us to grow and blossom and expand the radiance of our Inner Garden.

One of my favourite ways to celebrate is to dance. I use dance to find the sacred in each moment. When I finish a chapter, or a piece of work, I dance to celebrate its completion. Similarly, if I have writers block, I put some music on the stereo, turn it up loud, and dance around my office. I celebrate that I am stuck, because I know that for me it's an important part of the creative process. Dancing fizzes me up, and at the same time grounds each experience in my body so that I can acknowledge the gift in it.

I invite you to celebrate. I invite you to celebrate like you have never celebrated before. I invite you to celebrate that your Divinity, in all its glory, is available to you in each and every moment. I invite you to become the fizzy elixir of life that inspires others to do the same. I invite you to acknowledge your highs and your lows, and to celebrate each and every one of them. In doing so, you become firmly rooted in your garden. You create a space where you can acknowledge your own internal seasons of death, rebirth, rejuvenation, and blossoming. I invite you to celebrate the resplendent radiance of your Inner Garden, whatever that may be, so that you can blossom, ever fuller, into your exquisite potential.

And finally, I invite you to celebrate, because after all your hard work, it is so much FUN!!!

Celebrate all aspects of your womanhood. The Creatrix, the Seductress, the Nurturer, the Wise Woman, the Giver and Receiver of Love, are but a few. Connect to the sacred in each one of them, and allow them to inform your soul. As women, we must celebrate ourselves, but we must also celebrate every woman that came before us, because without them there would be no garden. They are the protectors, the gardeners, and the harvesters that nurtured the soil, so that our individual seeds could be planted. Without them and their vision we would not be here. The responsibility lies with us to hold the vision, and plant the seeds for the next generation to come.

Once upon a time there was Woman. She lived in a cave at the edge of the world. From there, she tended daily to the fire of womanhood. She honoured every aspect of its being, and in return it fed her. The fire fed her with its passion, its creativity, its joy, its love, and its warmth. The fire fuelled her desires, and blessed her with the gift of alchemy. She was a wise woman, a goddess, a lover, a healer, and the keeper of the flame.

Oftentimes women would come to her cave; women whose fire had gone out, and who were in need of her attention. She would rekindle their fire from the dusty ashes that they carried within themselves. She would reunite them with their spark. And they would return to the world, having remembered the sacredness of their feminine soul.

When you celebrate, you not only celebrate yourself, but you celebrate all the women who came before you, who never let the flame go out. So in time, when you were ready, you could claim your fire, and walk with your passion, your aliveness, and your sense of beauty in this world. Celebrate your ancestors and your lineage. Celebrate that you are a Goddess, and as such are the feminine incarnation of the Divine. Celebrate, because in doing so we create a new lineage; a lineage of women who stand tall in the essence of their garden, and proudly proclaim to the world:

"I am Woman, and I am Whole."

Exercises

The following exercises are designed to help you celebrate both yourself and the universal lineage of women that you are part of.

I am Woman, and I am Whole

This is a gorgeous exercise that will root you firmly into your garden in a matter of minutes. Use it whenever you like, throughout the day. It is especially helpful if you find yourself in a situation that unsettles you.

- Stand tall, and take a few deep breaths all the way down into your womb.
- With your eyes open or closed, visualise all the women who have come before you, and tended to the flame of womanhood standing in a circle around you.
- Feel them pouring their support, their compassion, their love, and their wisdom, onto you.
- Say either to yourself, or out loud, while connecting with all these amazing women, "I am Woman, and I am Whole."
- Keep repeating "I am Woman, and I am Whole" until you feel the fire of womanhood, or all the radiance of your garden rising up inside of you.
- When you are full of this energy, make a physical gesture that anchors this energy into your body. You could click your fingers, stamp your foot, toss your hair, wiggle your bum; whatever feels right to you.
- Whenever you want to reconnect to this energy simply repeat your physical gesture and say "I am Woman, and I am Whole."

Inner Garden Altar

Preparing and tending to an altar is a very old custom practiced by many tribal communities. An altar is a sacred place inside or outside your home, designed for the purpose of honouring. You may honour friends or loved ones that have passed on. You may choose to honour a particular deity, such as the earth, Buddha, a god or goddess, etc. whose energy you wish to bless your home and your life. In some instances, altars are used to represent externally that which you wish to nurture and celebrate internally. It is this aspect of an altar that I invite you to experience. I invite you to create a living, breathing 3D manifestation of your Inner Garden.

Firstly, choose a place in your house where your altar will not be disturbed. You may choose to use the top of a dressing table, a small table in your bedroom, etc.

Gather objects that embody the aspects of your Inner Garden that you wish to honour and celebrate. Have fun with it. Use any items that represent your inner garden.

Some examples of objects you could use are:

- Candles
- Fresh flowers
- A picture of a garden
- A picture of yourself.
- Pictures of women that you admire

- Pictures of some of the women from your 'tribe'.
- Scented oils.
- Statue of a woman / goddess.
- Incense.
- Heart shape chocolates or crystals.
- Items from nature that you like; shells, stones, feathers, etc.
- A bottle of champagne.
- Poetry, etc.

Each day take a little time to be with your altar so that you can celebrate your Inner Garden. Remember to tend to it lovingly, keeping it free from dust and grime. As you change, you can change your altar, replacing some items with new ones that allow you to celebrate each new aspect of your garden as it emerges. Have fun with it. This is a celebration. It should not be work. The more you enjoy it, the more celebratory an experience it will be.

The Keeper of the Flame

Share what you have learned in this book with other women. In this way you become the keeper of the flame for other women in your life. It also allows you to continually celebrate and nurture you own Inner Garden.

The Grand Finale

Throw a party for yourself to celebrate your Womanhood. Invite other women along who play an important part in your life, so that you can celebrate your womanhood together. You may wish to invite participants to bring a poem, a song, a story, or something that they have created, which celebrates the different aspects of woman. Celebrate each other, and celebrate the divine blessing that you are all so different and yet the same. You are all radiant, fragrant beings, honouring and celebrating your Inner Garden.

Back into the Garden

This is a beautiful meditation to help you to reconnect with, and deepen, your connection to the energy of the garden. It is a perfect meditation to do if you are feeling disconnected from your Inner Garden, as it returns you to source, and allows you to birth yourself into the world anew. This meditation is also a lovely way to remember that you are an aspect of the Divine.

- Make yourself comfortable, allow your body to be loose, and start to breathe.
- Using your breath, centre yourself by breathing down your legs, and into the ground.

- As you breathe, connect to the childlike wonderment that lives inside you.
- Allow your imagination to take you to a garden paradise that is beautiful beyond your wildest dreams. There may be trees, laden with the juiciest of fruits; nature, teeming with the fullness of her lushness and abundance; animals, living in balance and harmony, etc.
- Visualise the iridescence of the colours; the pungency of the smells. Listen and sense the sheer aliveness of everything that is present in this place.
- Begin to walk through this beautiful place, fully engaging all your senses as you do so. What can you hear? What do you see? What does this place feel like to the touch? What can you taste? What can you smell?
- As you walk, you reach the Point of Creation. This is the Point of Inception, where you first came into being. In other words, you were birthed from this place. This beautiful abundant place was the womb where your soul gestated, held in the arms of the Divine.
- Rest here, and feel that you are connected to everything. You are the garden, the lushness, the beauty, and the abundance. You are not separated from the Divine. You are a beautiful part of it.
- Become aware that your gestation period is drawing to

an end. You begin to feel yourself been drawn down into the birth canal. There is nothing to worry about. You are completely safe. As you move down the birth canal you stay completely connected to the energy of this beautiful garden paradise. You are shrouded in this lovely energy, and you are always held in the arms of the Divine.

- Your eyes are filled with the images of the garden, and you feel the garden energy alive in every cell of your being.

- Then, while still being held by all this beautiful energy, you are birthed into the world. You take a gorgeous breath of air. As you breathe, you can feel the garden still inside you. You can feel the Divine all around you. You see the Divinity in the eyes of all those now looking at you; mother, father, and midwife.

- As you breathe, you know that wherever you go in life, you are never separate from the garden. You are the garden, and she is You.

Acknowledgements

This book has been a labour of love and it would not have been birthed into the world without some amazing help along the way.

I am eternally grateful to Mary Ann Hylton who took me into her home and into her heart at a time when I was so badly broken, and changed my life for ever. I love you sweet lady.

I give thanks for my Warrior Women who have unrelenting faith in me, even when I sometimes lose faith in myself, Joanna Kossak Goddess Extraordinaire, Lynda Leech O'Duinn, Moira O'Reilly, Rita Fagan, Sally Baker and Trish Bonham Corcoran.

Huge thanks to Barbara Stanny for her ongoing support and for being my cheerleader, and to all my clients and students over the years, I have learned so much from each and every one of you.

Deep gratitude to Eddie O'Hanlon, Caroline Doyle and Breffni Smith for their generous help with the manuscript.

I give thanks for my family, and for all the women who have gone before me in remembering your stories, I heard my heartsong.

Soulful gratitude to Julie and Paul Dollman, master shamans, spiritual counsellors and above all, dearest friends. Anything is possible with you two by my side.

Heartfelt thanks to the two special men in my life. Aidan Walsh where would I be without you, you are the best pal a gal could ask for. And my Beloved Vincent, I give thanks everyday that you are in my life. My heart is open because of you and my days are filled with love and laughter. Thank you for believing in me so that I could believe in myself.

I am so grateful for the most amazing midwife, Lindy McDonnell at McZine for being the answer to my prayers and helping me birth this book from inside my laptop out into the world.

Eternal gratitude to Mother Earth and Great Spirit, for holding me close and guiding me each step of the way. It is an honour to be your daughter.

Acknowledgements

And to 'The Lads' my beloved guides. I am humbled by the faith you have put in me and all that you have shared with me over the years. I could not do the work I do without you, this was truly a match made in Heaven.

And to You, for reading this book, I hope that we get to meet often in the Garden.

About the Author

Catherine Maguire has been teaching personal empowerment for over 15 years. Her unique visionary gift of seeing her client's deep soul path comes with timeless wisdom and the ability to unlock her client's truest unique potential. She is a powerful shamanic practitioner, intuitive soul reader, workshop facilitator and inspirational change bringer. Her gifts create a dynamism that transforms those she works with forever. She is known for her honesty, her passion, her natural storytelling ability as well as her wisdom and her wicked sense of humour.

A former television executive, Catherine's wake up

call came in her late twenties when no matter how hard she worked, she couldn't run from the problems of her early childhood. Her subsequent breakdown and recovery caused an unlocking of the true talents that she had been resisting for years and a complete change in career. Because she has had to 'walk the talk' Catherine's bravery and empathy supports her clients in their metamorphosis.

She has trained in shamanism, tantra and relationship dynamics. She is a graduate of The Four Winds shamanic practitioners training, the Mastery Program at the School of Womanly Arts in New York, and the Soul Mate Tantra Training Program as the School of Awakening in the UK.

Catherine has travelled all over the world to sacred sites in the U.S.A, Hawaii, Peru, China and Mongolia to unearth the sacred teachings that she shares to empower her clients, reminding them of what is possible. She believes that to end the suffering in the world we must first end the suffering within ourselves, and she provides powerful, practical tools to help each individual make that possible.

She lives in the beautiful countryside of Co. Wicklow in Ireland. She draws deeply on the richness of the countryside in her work and frequently hosts shamanic gatherings, healing ceremonies, and women's wisdom circles on her land. *Tending to your Inner Garden* is her first book.